FLYING FUNNY

FLYING FUNNY

MY LIFE
WITHOUT A NET

Dudley Riggs

Foreword by Al Franken

University of Minnesota Press
Minneapolis
London

Published by the University of Minnesota Press
111 Third Avenue South, Suite 290
Minneapolis, MN 55401-2520
http://www.upress.umn.edu

ISBN 978-1-5179-0167-7 (hc)
ISBN 978-1-5179-0094-6 (pb)
A Cataloging-in-Publication record for this book is available from the Library of Congress.

Printed in the United States of America on acid-free paper

The University of Minnesota is an equal-opportunity educator and employer.

22 21 20 19 18 17   10 9 8 7 6 5 4 3 2 1

This book is for Pauline,
my closest friend and loving wife,
now for more than a third of a century.

CONTENTS

FOREWORD

Al Franken

In 1968, two geeky teenagers went to a show at a small revue theater in Minneapolis called Dudley Riggs' Brave New Workshop. The geekier of the two, me, was a senior in high school. The other, Tom Davis, was a junior. That night we saw adult people doing what we wanted to do: perform onstage and make people laugh.

Tom and I had been writing and performing at school, teaming up to do morning announcements for laughs. Obviously, we had watched comedians on television. But for some reason, seeing live comedy on a stage made show business seem like a real option for two kids from Minnesota.

After the show, the cast did an improv set based on audience suggestions. Some of the stuff worked, some of it didn't. But that's what made it even more exhilarating when the performers scored. Improv techniques were also developing at the more famous Second City in Chicago after it opened in 1959, and Tom and I often referred to Dudley's as Third City.

Tom and I kept returning for the improv sets, which were free. We quickly got to know the performers, who were really just a few years older than we were. After one of those sets, we met Dudley Riggs.

Dudley was an exotic figure for two suburban boys. He's actually an exotic figure, period. A former vaudevillian and circus performer, Dudley evoked Professor Marvel from *The Wizard of Oz*. Bow-tied, slightly rotund, jovial, and, at the time, I think, someone who enjoyed an alcoholic beverage or two or three, Dudley was one of the first larger-than-life characters I've been fortunate (and in one or two instances, unfortunate) to meet.

Dudley took an interest in me and Tom and invited us to get up onstage on what, at most comedy clubs, is called "open mic night." Except here the theater was so small there was no need for microphones. As a matter of fact, there were really no comedy clubs in America at that time. No places called The Punchline or Zanies or the Laugh Factory.

Tom and I got up on a Monday night—I think. I do remember getting laughs with our parody of a local newscast taking place on the night after the day of World War III. Dudley liked us and said he saw "sparks." Holy moly!

Before long, we were doing our own two-man show at the Workshop, getting not only notes from Dudley but also money. We were professional comedians!

But off I went to college. During the summers, Tom and I would do shows at the Workshop. I also had a day job, working for my suburb's street department, mowing grass and weeds around the water tower and other city property on an industrial-sized rider mower. The schedule started getting the best of me, and one night I got a terrible migraine before our show. I told Tom he might have to cover if I suddenly had to run backstage and throw up.

Fortunately, Tom had been working on a couple of monologues and pulled it off. The audience figured out what was going on and gave us a standing ovation at the end of the show. Dudley had been watching from the back of the house and came backstage to commend us. While I was lying facedown on a couch, Tom asked Dudley what would have happened if I'd thrown up on stage.

"The audience would have all left," he said with the absolute assurance of a grizzled show-business veteran.

In the fall, I'd go to college, and Tom joined the regular cast at the Workshop, becoming a hilarious improvisational performer. I regret that I never had that improv training that *Saturday Night Live* cast members from John Belushi, Jane Curtin, Bill Murray through to Will Ferrell, Amy Poehler, and Tina Fey were all steeped in.

At the end of the summer between my junior and senior years of college, Tom and I hitchhiked from Minneapolis to L.A. We stayed with Pat Proft, a Brave New Workshop alum, who went on to cowrite the *Naked Gun* movies, the *Police Academy* movies, and tons of others. Pat got us a slot at The Comedy Store, a new stand-up club on the Sunset Strip, and suddenly our peers in the stand-up world knew who we were.

It was because Dudley recognized some "sparks" when we

were in high school that Tom and I became Franken and Davis. After becoming writer/performers on *SNL*, we kept returning to Dudley's to work out material that would find its way on the show.

Dudley couldn't have been prouder of us. And I couldn't be prouder of being an alum of his theater and a friend.

FLYING FUNNY

I rosin my hands after I'm up the ladder. That way, none is lost in the climb. Besides, the ritual of powdering my hands builds audience anticipation. We buy solid rosin blocks at a music store. The deep amber intended for the bows of cellos and violins is crushed and placed in a clean white sock to become a rosin powder bag that makes my hands sticky and improves my grip.

As I prepare to fly, I focus on the little details, almost unaware of the crowd—the big picture—what I'm about to do. Then I release my feet from the platform, hop tall, point my toes, and fly. Now I feel the rush, the aliveness, the arousal, and the fun of flying.

Aerial acrobatics do not feel the way they appear to the audience. I do not see myself at this moment as a figure fluidly passing from one trapeze and flying into the hands of another man swinging in the air. Instead, I concentrate on getting pumped, on getting plenty of air before taking the fly bar. The fly bar is heavy—a solid rod of steel—and when you take the bar it has energy, you have to be ready to go—it could pull you right off the pedestal if your balance fails. When the catcher wraps his legs into a Dutch Lock, I know it's time. The catcher swings out and back, two swings to complete the geometry of my one longer arc. When he's at the near end of his swing, "it's showtime," and I must go down the hill of space and meet him as he comes up to take my wrists.

It is surprisingly easy to forget the way it must look to the audience, the way it must feel to someone watching as we risk death for a living. The flying trapeze remains the most graceful, romantic act in the circus, and after many years of flying, I'm still a little astonished when I see someone else performing in a great flying act.

People are afraid of the unknown. Most people have a fear of falling. But flyers need to believe that is a learned fear. We don't climb the circus ladder in fear. Gravity is a known constant—gravity is reliable—always there to power my swing. We aren't nuts up there; we do have a respect for gravity.

And so when I take these steps, I climb the rope ladder, heels first, pressing against the sides to maintain tension. It's what I know. Just as I know at what point my hands might start to sweat and defeat my grip. I know when I reach the top how to retrieve the bar, find the spot to stand, how far to lean back on the lines. I know these steps to the point that I don't have to think about them anymore; it's in my head and muscle memory. I'm not thinking, "Can I do this?" I'm thinking, "Hey, watch this!"

"Breathe positive and enjoy the moment," Doc always said. Doc was my teacher, my trapeze partner, and my dad. "You are working for that moment when the crowd gasps, then cheers, the moment when fear gives way to exhilaration," he said. "Face it, Son, flying is sexy."

And risky. Pride plays an illusive role in the circus; arrogant pride can get you killed. You just don't want to get too cocky. Just when you think you are the best, chances are you'll blow it; you are not the best once you think you are—kind of a paradox, right? Flying tricks require subtle confidence and, of course, faith in what you are doing. You also need to remember why you're up there: to entertain the public, to enjoy doing what they can't do.

A flyer must have pride in his passes and faith in the catcher. The catcher is the one who really makes the act. A good catcher is valuable beyond measure, someone who just might save your life. He is someone who can straighten you out, untangle a mess you've made of a trick, and get you safely back to the bar so that you can take the applause.

"You are too tall to ever be a great flyer," my flying coach, Freddy Valentine, once told me. "Your height works for you in the horizontal bar act—but for the flying act, you're too tall to ball up in your tuck." Fred, an old-time flyer, was wise and very honest. "Look, you can fly funny, all flailing arms and crazy legs, but you're too damn tall to fly straight. Stick with comedy."

Eventually I had to decide: to fly or be funny. Improvisational theater turned out to be both.

INTRODUCTION

"Show business is America, America is show business," Billy Rose, the great showman, liked to say. Today, when show business is such a vast enterprise, it's hard to believe there was a time when show business outside of the major cities meant only "variety show business": vaudeville and the circus. All manners of entertainment—from dancers, acrobats, and jugglers to contortionists and hand balancers—performed with music but often without words. Silent, pantomime acts— "dumb acts"—were interspersed with singers, actors, and comedians. "Novelty acts," a term that stripped away an act's claim to ever be considered important, fit under the banner of "variety."

Variety acts so dominated the field of vaudeville entertainment that the trade journal for show business was and is still named *Variety*. Of course, in big cities, there was also legit theater and opera, which offered high prestige, but often paid a lot less. Some stars found themselves taking home more money in Peoria than they could in New York. It was okay to brag about your European tour, but not a good idea to talk up those twelve weeks playing small houses in all of those inland states where most of America's food comes from.

My parents were performing in vaudeville in Little Rock, Arkansas, when I was born. My crib was a hotel dresser drawer, and my nanny was Albert White (known as Flo), a male–female clown. As soon as I was able to sit up, they cast me in the circus—parading in a pony cart. My life in show business began.

So far I've had three show business careers. In my adult life, I produced and directed more than 250 original live theatrical productions at Dudley Riggs' Brave New Workshop. Known as the nation's oldest ongoing satirical comedy theater, Brave New Workshop still today presents social and political satire in revue format year-round. Many of America's greatest comedy artists, writers, actors, and producers learned the art of improvisation on my stage before going on to fame and fortune.

That list is long. It includes Louie Anderson, Avner the Eccentric, Del Close, Mo Collins, The Flying Karamazov Brothers, Franken & Davis, Lorna Landvik, Carl Lumbly, Peter MacNicol, Pat Proft, Penn & Teller, Stevie Ray, Sue Scott, Rich Sommer, Nancy Steen, Steven Schaubel, Faith Sullivan, Peter Tolan, Linda Wallem, and Lizz Winstead. The theater—now known as the Brave New Workshop Comedy Theater—continues to make me proud. But these years spent producing and directing at the Brave New Workshop were actually my *third* career.

My *first* career was as a child star in vaudeville, and my *second* was as a fearless circus flyer. I performed for the Russell Brothers Circus, the Blackpool Tower Circus (England), Cirko Grande (Havana, Cuba), the Al G. Kelly & Miller Brothers Circus (USA), Stevens Brothers Circus (USA), the Dolly Jacobs Circus (Canada and Alaska), the E. K. Fernandez All-American Circus (Japan), and the Grande Cirko Americano (Puerto Rico). In vaudeville, I performed on the Barnes and Caruthers, Shubert, and Sacco entertainment circuits, throughout the United States.

I had loving parents, helpful uncles, and a grande dame of a Victorian grandmother who would only bring out her crystal ball if other family members couldn't get work. Adults treated me like an equal, as long as I hit my mark on cue. Because my family was always on the road, I never had a hometown. For me, "home" was where the work was.

I grew up listening to nineteenth-century circus music, abiding by the rules of the highly organized, glamorous, immensely complicated business that thrives on tradition, wondrous hyperbole, and the command of the ringmaster. The circus runs on rules.

In college I discovered and became overly fond of modern jazz, which seemed above rules. My mind's ear was filled with jazz and circus music but crowded by a stubborn, recurrent notion I had of creating an original scene onstage while performing it.

"Theater without a script," created by the actors through "free association," was a concept from psychotherapy just entering my thinking in the 1950s. This would be theater of words not memorized from a script written by someone else or from some other time and place, but words discovered by the actors themselves. Words made up spontaneously *in* performance, not contrived in advance *for* performance. People said . . . *that's an insane idea.*

It took time, crazy dedication, and a few evictions to build an audience for this new kind of theater. It took actors willing to trust me, take the risk, listen, cooperate, and trust their talent. Actors who want to work this way are finding places that encourage them now, but we went through a long phase when actors were screaming inside for an audience but had no place to perform. What actually started out as a tool to cover stage waits in vaudeville and control drunks in a nightclub audience became a new way to communicate and entertain.

My life has been constantly in motion, toward mostly unplanned goals: testing, evolving, curious about the next surprise. Happily seeking satirical targets and exposing vice and folly. Always looking for fresh minds, talented artists, new ideas, and astonishment. Keeping my "suitcase act" always at the ready.

What follows is the story of a boy growing up in the rigid tradition of the circus and in vaudeville, and the unconventional education that prepared him for forty years of producing comedy theater, experimenting, and eventually developing a way to work improvisationally.

It would seem an unlikely path to travel from the exacting traditions of the well-ordered circus to the "no rules" philosophy of the improvisational stage. But both must entertain. And start on time.

★ 1 ★

THE POLAR PRINCE

The amazing aerial artists, Riggs & Riggs, performed their uniquely romantic, and dangerous pas de deux on the high trapeze. This young married couple has toured in circuses internationally, always with top billing and income, striving to be the best double trapeze act in the world. In America they are always placed high over the center ring.

— NEW YORK POST, APRIL 11, 1928

I was born as planned during the off-season. My arrival on the coldest day in January 1932—in the bottom year of the Great Depression—was a conscious, perhaps imprudent, decision on my parents' part after five years of marriage during bad economic times. I know all of this because of my mother's constant reminder: "Always remember, you were born a very much wanted child."

I was soon touring the country with the Russell Brothers Circus, a large motorized circus, a big "mud show." It was one of many such shows during the golden age of circus. In the

1930s and 1940s there were dozens of circuses in America, all smaller than the Ringling Brothers or Cole Brothers, but by no means tiny. They all had the requisite three rings expected by the public with lions, tigers, elephants, and clowns. A great American tradition, mud shows brought education and entertainment to the small towns that were passed over by the grand railroad-mounted circuses. My folks originated a beautiful but risky high aerial double trapeze act performed forty feet in the air without a net. The announcer proclaimed "beauty and danger aloft"—so that all eyes would be on Riggs & Riggs.

My parents, lacking a regular babysitter, decided to keep track of me by putting me in the show. Management outfitted a little wagon pulled by a tiny canyon pony (a horse breed thirty-four inches high) that was led around the hippodrome track in the opening spectacle. Before the season was over, my parents upgraded my tour of the track, replacing the pony with a muzzled polar bear cub pulling a wheeled sleigh, and I was dressed in a fur cape and a crown. I was presented, in circus hyperbole, as the Polar Prince from the North Pole. When we hit hot weather, the polar bear, which couldn't tolerate the ninety-degree weather, went nuts! So we went back to using the pony—but they kept me in the hot fur robe. All I remember is what I was told—and that the polar bear deserved better treatment.

Russell Brothers was a national show, but like many of the motorized shows, tended not to go farther west than Denver because of the difficulty of getting heavy trucks and elephants over the Rocky Mountains. In 1940 we owned our own show—the Riggs Brothers Circus—which ironically grew larger as economic times got leaner. When Ringling Brothers and Barnum & Bailey closed early in the bottom of the Depression, many of their acts joined the Riggs Brothers Circus in order to survive. We provided unemployed performers with a "cookhouse" and feed for their animals. (Otherwise, exotic livestock from failing circus companies would have had to be given to a zoo, or shot.)

We toured from Cleveland to Denver, Michigan to Texas, and sometimes down to Mexico in the winter. The Riggs Brothers Circus had a longer season and, unlike other circuses, we had no "winter quarters." A homeless Riggs Brothers Circus operated year-round, providing jobs and entertainment nonstop because we simply never had enough cash to close. This was a policy I would draw upon later with the Brave New Workshop, when we kept our doors open fifty-two weeks a year.

Doc always said, "We do not cancel performances." I quickly learned that if you stop moving, the cash stops flowing. That may be the real reason show people always say "the show must go on."

I did not call my father "Dad" or "Father" until the last years of his life. Dudley Henry Riggs Sr. was always known as "Doc," and my mother as "Lil." Doc got that name when a confused Texas state trooper misread the enlarged "D" and "R" on a circus promotional flyer and of course assumed that "DR" meant that my dad was a doctor. He had also appeared in a risqué doctor sketch in vaudeville, the "Oh, Doctor!" sketch that had been part of the Riggs family repertoire for three generations. Fans of the act often called out the punch line "Oh, Doctor!" to my dad on the street. The name stuck, and as a result I was sometimes referred to as "Little Doc."

Doc Riggs worked in the circus for at least part of every season from his teens until his death. In his last years he was developing young comic talents at the Clown College in Florida, and still inventing funny props. Throughout his life he kept working on showbiz skills that he said he could fall back on during slow times or the off-season. He had been a machinist, a carpenter, a sign painter, an actor, a talent salesman, and even a movie stand-in for Clark Gable. Show people tend to gripe a lot, always threatening to quit the business, but no matter what they say, most do strive to stay in "the show business." They hate having to work civilian jobs. Non-show work was not something you bragged about, but sometimes it was necessary to pay for food or the dentist.

"Show business is ephemeral," said Grandmother Riggs. "We live for that great moment of excitement and pleasure when the applause is in balance with the sacrifice and years of hard work spent preparing for that moment. That's why we love show business."

A life in show business seemed to be what everyone around me wanted, and I wanted it too. But it wasn't that easy. As Grandmother Riggs would tell me: "You need to maintain and polish your special gift of talent." Her statements over the years were almost scriptural.

And Doc always said, "Everyone should have a suitcase act, in case an opportunity to entertain should arise."

Circus tradition demands having something to fall back on:

a second act immediately available if or when the audience (or an agent) asks, "What else can you do?" I have personally never felt safe enough to discard my old "suitcase act." Even now, in supposed retirement, a full dress suit, top hat, and fire juggling torches are here in the little red suitcase.

My dad had also been born to a show business family. His grandfather, James Riggs, had served in the British Cavalry, and after his discharge had become a trainer of horses for the circus. His son, Frank, my grandfather, also worked in the circus as a hand balancer, contortionist, and acrobat. Some years later, Frank left British show business and emigrated through Canada to the United States, where the original Riggs family revue was founded. The original act started with Frank; his wife, Emma Peabody Riggs; and their three sons, Arthur, Albert, and my father, Dudley Sr. By 1915, the act was billed as The Riggs Brothers no matter which of the three "brothers" were in it. Over the years, the act would become just my father, by then known as Doc, and my mother Lil, billed as Riggs & Riggs: Those Different Acrobats. But the original name would live on—years later, when my dad and I had our own act, we were still called The Riggs Brothers.

My parents met when Lillian, who was just out of business college, took a summer job as a magician's assistant with The Great Cardini's traveling magic show. Cardini, a popular magician in vaudeville, was best known for his card tricks but could also make an elephant disappear from the stage. My mom was featured in Cardini's popular Dollhouse act. At four feet eleven inches and ninety pounds, and very limber, she was a perfect subject, able to bend and contort her body enough to secretly fit into the two-foot-square glass "dollhouse" that appeared to be empty. At the end of the act, Cardini would say, "Such a lovely dollhouse needs a little doll," whereupon my mother (having waited so patiently and compactly for an hour) would pop out of the house on cue—a visual punch line to Cardini's act.

Cardini's bookings overlapped with the Riggs family's bookings in the late 1920s, and my parents met when their shows "day and dated"—which meant both had shows at the same time and city—in this case, New York City. Doc courted Lil for the better part of the season, while Grandmother Riggs maintained a firm, Victorian hand to assure propriety. They were married in 1927—he was twenty-four, she was eighteen—a banner era for vaudeville, but that ended when the stock market crashed two years later.

Although my mother was called Lillian, her real name was Martha Julily Harker. She *said* she was born in Missouri in 1911, although it must have been earlier. She had a tendency to be vague about her age and her background. Her parents died when she was very young, and she was brought up by her older brothers and sisters. She was the youngest by far in an immigrant family that left in Germany in the nineteenth century.

Lil was tiny but strong, with what was then called a "perfect thirty-six" figure (thirty-six-inch bust, tiny waist, and thirty-six-inch hips). In the hand-balancing act, she would do a backbend, her hands and feet within one square foot on the floor, thereby creating a platform for my father's handstand.

This was their startling opening move—the statuesque man balanced on the tiny woman—that always got great applause and top billing.

My mother had what was then called Jean Harlow hair—wavy platinum blond, which was the current fashion—and she liked diamonds. She was even billed for a while as Diamond Lil. She always dressed fashionably with as much gold and as many diamonds as she could afford, which varied with the state of the family economy.

Grandmother Riggs was my closest friend and confidant, always wise and loving. She taught me what it meant to "be a Riggs." Grandmother Riggs was always rather formally dressed—Victorian long dresses, tall collars—and she traveled with a padded, black leather case with a full Wedgwood tea service. Oddly, while she always insisted on a high standard of good and proper behavior, she was amazingly candid and open-minded. "Remember: Noblesse oblige—we must have respect for the others."

Grandmother Riggs would often take me to Caffé Reggio, an espresso shop in Greenwich Village, for a treat. She taught me how to spoon a little coffee over my ice cream and would offer advice on how to handle my parents, such as the time when I had just turned eight, had lost my job in the family vaudeville act, and was getting cranky. She also used such occasions to teach me further lessons in what it meant to "be a Riggs," such as explaining why we always dressed up for dinner. "We have a standard of comportment: A young gentleman stands when a lady enters the room. Know that you are always in the public spotlight, so you must remember at all times to choose an honorable path. Have respect for the problems of others. You cannot control what others do, but we have our standards. Remember: Noblesse oblige."

Grandmother Riggs also performed for the family vaudeville act. She denied being a clairvoyant, but she did have some abilities that authenticated her to work as a "stage mentalist." She was very shy about her gifts and would perform reluctantly, only when the family needed money.

"I do not make predictions. I'm not Nostradamus. But sometimes I seem to know when an event happens without benefit of any real information. I'm not sure how, but I knew instantly when my son, Al, had been hurt in an automobile crash a thousand miles away."

When family finances required her performance, she would allow our agent to book her "mentalist" act. Onstage, she would hold up a crystal ball and say in a commanding voice, "I own but do not *use* a crystal ball because I *do not believe* in magic. I show it to you only because you all *expect* to see a crystal ball." (She loved sending up the crowd.) "I am not a gypsy, I am not a fortune-teller, I am not a magician. What I do, I do without trickery and without any help from the devil." An Episcopalian by birth, she said she was a rationalist by choice.

Using the stage name Madame Emma, my grandmother would then astonish the audience by what she called mathematical memory skills. For example, she would ask for twenty-five volunteers to join her onstage and ask each of them to recite their date of birth, one after the other, like a roll call. She would then walk past each person and state what day of the week they were born. As the subjects verified that she got that one right, she would then turn to the audience and announce numbers that were the total years and days that the twenty-five people had lived so far. A certified public accountant, recruited from the local bank, would use his adding machine to verify each segment of her performance.

Grandmother—Madame Emma—would then ask the audience members to shout out their names and Social Security numbers. (It was a more innocent time.) As the numbers were called out, she would write them on the blackboard, stacking the numbers wherever there was room on the board. On the twenty-fifth number she would, with a grand flourish, instantly write down a number that was the sum total of all twenty-five Social Security numbers. The CPA with his adding machine would take an extra minute or two to catch up with the same total.

She was authoritative but also privately humble. "My only gift is that I have a good memory," she would say afterward, and she meant it. That only heightened the sense of mystery and the aura of invisible power she conveyed. In her last days on her dying bed, she rejected the hospital chaplain's offer of prayer, saying, "Heaven and hell exist only in the minds of the uncurious." She passed the crystal ball down to me when she died, but none of her powers came with it.

When I was little, my dad decided to cast me in a perch act. It was a relatively easy act to build—an inch-and-a-half steel tube with a tricycle seat on top. So when I was quite young,

I think three years old, he put me up on a fourteen-footer. Later, as I got bigger, we went up to twenty-one feet, then thirty. I could shimmy up to the top of the pole, sit in the trike seat, and do a shoulder stand as Doc balanced the pole on his shoulder, his arms relaxed at his sides.

During one layover between shows, he arranged rehearsal time during the off-hours at a cement block factory, a building that had the necessary high ceiling. Seated on top of the pole, after a while, I became childishly fascinated with all of the belts and motors bolted to the ceiling of the factory. I became so absorbed that I lost my concentration, leaned out to touch a bright belt, and tilted the pole dangerously. As the pole fell, Doc caught me safely and held me tight for a long time. "You must learn from falling, Son," he said. "Never forget how hard the cement is." I never forgot what Doc said: "Remember what you learn from falling." *Gravity is reliable. Falling is possible.* But I'd felt safe and protected even after this first experience with falling.

When Doc and I had the perch act, a few people commented that my parents were putting a child at risk up on top of a tall pole. But I performed under high scrutiny, spotted by my mother, and while it's conceivable that I could have been hurt, the risk was pretty minimal. My dad was very strong and capable of keeping me safe. If he had chosen to balance a dozen eggs up there, everyone would have said, "Gee, he didn't break any of the eggs." Nor did he break his little son. For a season or two, it was one of the family's regular acts.

I never doubted my father's love and his ability to protect me. When I was six, he punched out and fired a clown who made a predatory move toward me. At ten, I grew into the flying trapeze act, and he never missed a catch. He always spotted my comedy pratfalls and eased my teenage doubts. Once I could pass as an adult, we billed ourselves professionally as "The Riggs Brothers," dressed alike, and presented ourselves, professionally and socially, as fun-loving bachelors. I thought it made me sound older and made Doc seem younger.

We were in an uncertain business, although the good times always seemed to rescue the bad. As a kid, I was never very aware of money problems because the adults didn't want to bother me with something I wouldn't understand. But sometimes there were signs that even a kid could figure out, like when we started reusing makeup towels, put fewer flowers in the dressing room, or started eating "in" instead of going to the usual restaurants.

In slow times, when the audiences were small, Doc would often go off alone with his trombone, find a back room someplace, and do a solo concert for himself. He would play "Paper Doll" over and over.

"If things don't pick up pretty soon, your dad will have to get a new song," my mother would say. "He's got that one down perfectly."

"Your dad is a self-taught musician," Grandmother would add. "Ten instruments and never a single lesson." She was such a solid woman, always serene and apparently happy—she always managed to see the bright side, even when times were bad.

Doc was different. When things were booming, he'd get worried, and when times got tight, he remained optimistic. He saw the same picture as Grandmother Riggs, but backwards. If we had a standing-room-only business, he would run out, all over the theater, checking the exits. "You never know when someone might panic and yell 'Fire!' when they see the fire jugglers' finale!" He was always anticipating trouble, always looking out for potential grief.

This drove my mother frantic. She would savor a down mood for an hour and then "be up and at 'em," looking for an active thing to do.

For show people, cash was always a problem. Our contracts always stated that "the fee must be paid to the performers no later than intermission." No fee, no second act. Because performers couldn't always depend on being paid—the check might not be good—it was common for the fee to be demanded in cash. When you're on the road all the time, and not developing much trust or credit, and lacking a friendly hometown bank, you end up being forced to carry greenbacks. Transporting cash has its risks, but sometimes cash does talk. When times were good, Lil bought a new car each fall, and almost always paid the wholesale price for it with hundred-dollar bills.

When we traveled by train, she required three steamer trunks, one just for shoes—a bone of contention with my father when money was thin. Grandmother Riggs always taught the Victorian philosophy of "nothing to excess." She encouraged "moderation in all things," and this included shoes, alcohol, and ice cream. These two very strong, very different women always got along well, however, because they shared what they called a common problem—my father. He could never satisfy them both, but he never stopped trying.

When they were first married and in vaudeville, Doc and Lil performed as Riggs & Riggs. They had equal billing and equal pay—there was no hierarchy between them. The idea of equality was important to my folks early on, and the division of labor was pretty well shared. Doc took a great deal of pride in the fact that we were an "American act," distinguishing ourselves from the European acts, where brothers having control over sisters, and husbands over wives was the norm. In our family, that was bad form. Years later, I was proud to run one of the first theaters committed to equal opportunity.

After a half century of performing, of diving off seventy-foot-high boards, flying through the air, and supporting my mother on the palm of his hand, Doc remained physically strong into his old age. In the circus aerial work, he and I developed strong shoulders and upper bodies more so than our legs.

My Uncle Art, on the other hand, was a ballet dancer with marvelously developed legs. My mother always said that Art had better-looking legs than most of the women in the show. When Art appeared with my parents, he performed some very muscular tricks—dressed as a woman. After an especially strenuous series of steps, he would take a ladylike bow, then remove his wig and pull down his top to take a second bow as a hairy-chested man. The audience howled.

In the fall and winter—the circus off-season—we were often booked into nightclubs or vaudeville theaters like the Oriental in Chicago or the Music Hall in New York. The vaudeville theater season started in the fall—because in those days there was little to no air conditioning, and theaters were too hot in the summer. My parents did a "low" version of their circus aerial act in these theaters, fifteen or twenty feet high instead of the forty to fifty feet in the circus tent. If you had a circus act and you wanted to get work year-round, you had to make the act available to work indoors, as well as in a tent.

Our fortunes were never very predictable. We had to go where the work was. And we put on a lot of miles getting to some engagements that didn't last. Doc painted a lot of signs in exchange for gas money. The Riggs & Riggs Double Trapeze Act was, however, always a center-ring presentation. Working without a net, the act always held the full attention of the audience and most of the other performers, who would watch Doc and Lil perform. But I had a better view of the act. Wearing a matching costume, I worked in the ring *under* their trapeze to "stand" the act where I could hopefully help them if they fell. I watched my parents risk their lives directly over my head night after night. I was nine years old.

Home for me was truly where the work was. If there was any time off at all, we would try to spend it as close as possible to where the next job would be. "The first rule of success in show business," said Doc, "is show up on time."

Traveling continually, our living conditions were almost always temporary. Sometimes we would get into an apartment for a month or two. Often, we'd buy a house, live in it for a few weeks, then lease it to someone else, and not live in it again. I was never in any of these houses long enough to claim a space as "my room." At one time Lil was making mortgage payments on three houses we were not living in. Mother always said that someday she'd like to stay put, "at least for a while."

But she couldn't seem to decide where. So our suitcases stayed packed year after year.

When we played the Boston Garden, it was just another building to me. What makes these venues distinctive for local audiences is quite different from what makes them distinctive to us as performers. I remember many buildings we played based on how hard they were to rig, where the girders were, where the dressing rooms were located—a lot of these auditoriums and theaters were designed by contractors, not by artists. So, out of some two hundred towns a year—Peoria, Iberia, Kansas City, name any town—the things I remember are quite mundane, other than maybe if the audience was exceptionally wonderful, or if we had bad weather, or if there was some big crowd or catastrophe. In my mind now, all the towns merge into *one big town.* Sometimes I found myself in the awkward situation of having to ask a local citizen, "Excuse me, but what town am I in?" To them it was a crazy question, but not if you are a kid and you've been in a different "new" town every day week after week.

The circus played mostly one-night stands. We had to load and unload daily. If there was a layoff, we'd still stay packed, ready to move all the time. Whenever there was a lull in the bookings, I'd get to go to school. Because I grew up without a hometown and without schoolmates or what could be called a hometown "team," I never knew life as a "towner" and therefore never missed it.

Another consequence of life on the road for an only child was that I spent my time primarily with adults. I can remember maybe a couple of names of kids from seventh grade when

I got to spend all of four months at school between jobs. And there were people I met much later in college, but it's a very small list. For show kids, usually the only other kids you see are the ones in the audience. You can make them laugh, sigh, or gasp with delight, but you never get to know who they really are.

To other performers, I was neither quite a child nor quite an adult. All through my life Mother kept telling me never to forget that I was special. Years later she was still reminding me of that fact, even as I was married and the father of my own "very much wanted child." My grandmother and my two uncles were always kind and loving, and they treated me like an equal, grown-up member of the troupe. As long as I didn't blow a cue or talk too loud, I was welcome with the grown-ups. By the time I was a teenager, I had been treated like an adult for so long I thought I was one.

There were other oddities that made my family life the reversed mirror image of a "normal" family's. I grew up thinking that anybody not working on Christmas and New Year's was a failure. "If you ain't working on New Year's Eve, you ain't in show business." That was the way Shorty Lynn dismissed a lot of acts that were just trying to get a start in the business. "If you're not even good enough to get holiday bookings, then it looks like you have nothing to offer. Anybody who's anybody in this business works on New Year's Eve!"

The Riggs family always had steady work during the holidays and because all of the family birthdays fell in January— family planning for circus folks meant that babies arrived during the slow period after the New Year—we usually had all of the birthdays and all of the holiday gift rituals on the first open Monday after January 24, my mother's birthday and the usual turnaround day for vaude bookings. I always thought that combining it all into one day saved our family some of the painful holiday frustration that overwhelms so many civilian families.

"We work so that the audience can enjoy their day off," Grandmother Riggs said. "Christmas week is when the audience has time to experience some theatrical magic and to be transformed by art." So that's why we were doing five shows a day. Business is always great during the holidays.

There were exceptions, however. For three generations the Riggs clan had kept a "Daily Route Book," recording attendance, weather, and one or two sentences describing the "circumstances," "conditions," and the "social, political, and religious atmosphere." On one page Doc had written, "The two *quietest* weeks in show business are Christmas and Minneapolis." Now I live in Minneapolis, but it's no longer quiet.

VAUDEVILLE

*We are in Variety show business. We do a Variety Act,
sometimes referred to as a Novelty Act, sometimes as a
Dumb Act. We are not singers or actors, although sometimes
we sing and sometimes we act, most of our act is musically
accompanied pantomime. Sometimes what we do is called
a sight act. The Riggs Family has been performing this
kind of entertainment for three generations.*

—FRANK RIGGS, IN A LETTER TO THE
WILLIAM MORRIS AGENCY, 1925

*In vaudeville, with twelve good minutes, you can work
for a lifetime and never have to change your act.*

—EDDIE CANTOR

I received my Social Security card in 1937 at age five when
I was cast in a new vaudeville act singing "Benny's from
Heaven." It happened this way: when the Dematsiatsy Dance
Troupe lost their lead dancer because of a groin injury, our ad-
vertised fifteen acts of variety entertainment ended up short-

billed. The Riggs bankroll was also short, and our agent, Jack Roddy, needed something new. So they put me to work. In three weeks of between-show rehearsal, I learned how to sing a parody song, dance one new routine, and polished both a comic and a proper bow. Roddy sent me to the wardrobe lady, who built me a new full-dress suit and lined an oversized top hat with enough felt to fit me. A musical parody of "Pennies from Heaven," scored for my five-year-old vocal range, was rehearsed for as many hours as Grandmother Riggs and Mr. Petrillo's union would allow.

"Remember, let the song sing *you*," the music director kept saying. "The song will carry you home. Just keep your wind up and hit the back row of the balcony." A place was found for me on the bill, a good spot right after Nikko, the Wonder Dog. I opened in a very tight pin spot, lighting only my face and the top hat to conceal my size and child identity. The first part was a spoken intro with the band vamping to the tune of "Pennies from Heaven." I remember these words still today:

There was a traveling salesman by the name of Spear,
Who had been away from home, for exactly one year.
When he returned home, he found his wife Jennie
Had a babe in her arms, and she called him Benny.

This always got a laugh, and then, with full spotlight, I sang:

Now every time he asked she said, Benny's from heaven.
Her face turned red but still she said, Benny's from
    heaven.

I would do a circle step, eight, back to center, and then continue singing in my strongest, very deepest voice:

I've asked the neighbors all over town,
They don't remember little Benny's falling down.
If it wasn't for my pride, he said, I wouldn't bother.
But what I know about kids, I know, Benny must have
    a father.

After another laugh, I would sing in my normal five-year-old register, while the band put a big brass finish on it:

So when I look at Benny, it's plain as can be,
That Benny's from heaven, but he's not from me.

I held the last note for a long time.

Three and a half minutes slipped into a vaudeville lineup, a novelty song, sung by a little boy. To Jack Roddy's surprise, I was a hit. A man never quick to give compliments, Roddy said, "It isn't much, but someone might like it." Many did. It was so popular the stage manager moved me to the third from closing spot in the show.

Roddy, who was our agent for many years, called it "a sympathy act" at first, but then one of the papers ran a two-inch "nothing story" about parody and satire (two words not often connected to show business success), and suddenly I was moved even higher in the bill, to the next-to-closing spot. Some of the audience was coming to see "the little kid who sings the adult song." All that rehearsal had paid off.

Grandmother Riggs questioned the taste of this kind of material, and she protested the "shameful exploitation of this child" to Roddy, but, as usual, he was able to con her by offering a little more money and a better dressing room. So now I had my own announcement in the show, my own billing, and a paycheck of my own (almost always deposited into what they called "Dudley's education fund").

Because Doc and Lil were on early in the same show, my mother was always there to get me dressed, made up, and warmed up for the act. And either she or Grandmother would provide support and "stand the act" in the wings and add to the applause and then tell me how great I was. It was pretty heady stuff for a five-year-old.

Each new booking moved me into a theater classier than the last, and with a bigger orchestra, and longer rehearsals. We polished my "three good minutes." Before long, they told me I was the "show's little star." I was in the big time of vaudeville. I thought it would last forever.

In vaudeville theater dressing rooms the air was always filled with powder and cigarette smoke. It smelled of perfume, sweat, Max Factor makeup, and sometimes gin. The rhinestones and spangles flashed light from the mirror lights onto the low ceiling, and most of the chorus girls treated me like a beloved pet. Even years later, as a ten- and eleven-year-old, I would stay in the dressing room and out of the way during their quick changes, as the girls went from being drum majorettes to "Rose Pettles" to "nude" to fully dressed again for the big closing Oriental number.

Backstage was like a birthday party all the time because my "birthday" got mentioned almost every show. After my final regular bow, the announcer would milk the audience with "Ladies and Gentlemen, today is this young man's sixth birthday, let's give him one more round of applause." He had me turning six until I was nearly nine.

"It's just show business, Dudley," Grandmother Riggs reminded me. "It's all make-believe. People come to the theater to forget their troubles, have a laugh, and stop worrying for a few hours. If they enjoy your song more because they think you are six or five or ten years old, what's the harm? Miss Celeste is several years older than her billing, and she hasn't been a 'Miss' for many years."

Everyone on the bill routinely showered me with candy, hugs, and toys—well, almost everyone. Mr. Flamarian, a famous trick-shot sharpshooter, was the only performer who cussed me out if I came into his dressing room. All the other acts, especially the distaff acts and the chorus girls, let me hang around their dressing room when they were changing, always in a hurry, talking about men, swapping advice and lipsticks, cleaning up after the show. I was learning a great deal about people and life.

Sometimes we would playfully powder each other's makeup, clapping hands with the powder puff, "applauding" our faces. A dozen pretty chorines would take turns playing innocently with Max Factor and me. They were exotically beautiful and healthy, and, as Mother said, "ripe." I was in love with them all, and I was constantly smothered with affection. Maybe I was a *little* spoiled.

I thought that I was a happy kid, although without any other children in the show, I really didn't have any comparison. From the stage, I viewed the kids in the audience as snotty Little Lord Fauntleroys. I thought *they* were the ones who were *really* spoiled rotten. As it turns out, they had something I was missing. But I didn't know what until years later.

Miss Celeste, a sultry singer from Paris who was our headliner, who didn't like men very much and who didn't like children at all, started griping backstage about how spoiled *I* was. Miss Celeste was our greenroom agitator. There seems to be one in every stage company.

"Mind your own affairs, if any," Grandmother Riggs told her. And then she reassured me: "Don't worry, there is nothing wrong with you being a little spoiled. People only knock you when they see you happier than they are."

And why wouldn't I be happy? At six, I had my own car. Well, it was actually a pedal car, a red Fire Chief car that the publicity company got as part of the promotion for the show. A picture taken of me in the car was used to advertise both the show and Radio Chief Toys. I could drive that car all over backstage, as long as I stayed away from the dressing rooms of Miss Celeste and "The Great Flamarian."

My mother warned me about Mr. Flamarian. "He doesn't like you," she said. "He doesn't like anyone or anything except gin and paregoric. Just stay away from him." Not knowing anything about opium or liquor, I asked, "But why doesn't he like me?"

She sat me down on her lap. "Dudley, you need to know that not everyone *has* to like you. Your dad loves you. Grandmother Riggs loves you. I love you. The ladies of the chorus love you; the audience in the seats all love you. We've got Flamarian outnumbered."

"What about Mr. Roddy?" I asked.

"He just *likes* you. You never use 'love' and 'agent' in the same sentence."

After my first season, mixed-race duets were becoming increasingly popular, so Roddy wanted to get me on the "black and tan" bandwagon. He kept most of the show intact but wanted to add another kid act without adding much to the nut. He pulled a teenage dancer out of the Crazy Legs Troupe and offered him and me an extra ten dollars a week to be in a second act. That's how Forrest Jackson and I ended up singing and dancing to "Me and My Shadow." I sang and danced; Forrest, who was black, danced as my shadow on the other side of the scrim. He was twice my age and could dance circles around me. (And he did!) On the shadow screen he looked ten feet tall. Through the magic of back lighting, our black and white full-dress suits appeared to reverse color as we replaced each other behind the scrim. My every gesture and dance step was matched perfectly by his, but then his steps grew progressively more complex, and he would add an extra step here and there so that by the end of the act, the shadow was stealing the scene.

It played well, but it was never the big hit that Roddy wanted. He got us sixteen weeks' work playing the East Coast wheel but couldn't get us booked down South. "It's because those damn crackers haven't heard that the Civil War is over," said Roddy.

Forrest and I were always put up in separate hotels and

rarely saw each other much before showtime. We both knew something about this was wrong—but it was 1939 in America and as kids we just "did the act." When it was time to renew contracts, Forrest left with the Crazy Legs Troupe and started dancing solo and making real money touring Europe, where I heard he stayed in the very best hotels. He and I worked more than three hundred performances together, but I never really got to know him. Vaudeville was an industry that was forever bragging about being new and ever-changing, but no one was doing much about social change. I would have to wait until I was running my own show to address the world I saw from the road as a performer. It may have been one of the reasons I *had* to have my own theater.

I was doing two shows a day, with three on Saturday. Grandma and my beloved tutor, Dolly, handled costumes and makeup. We were tending to business and had settled into the rhythm of the lineup and the mutual affection felt across the footlights. I loved performing, I loved the audience, and they loved me back. Some said even the critics almost liked it.

I was sure that this was the big time. The money was good, and I could brag that I had my own Social Security card, and everyone was constantly telling me how great I was. I got a raise to forty dollars per week. I began to believe that I was *it*. I started to think that I was the big audience draw, that I was the one single act that the public came to see. Admittedly, I was not the *star* of the show, but I thought that most likely I was the most unforgettable act in the entire production. Wrong!

When my "Benny's from Heaven" was pulled from the

show, I was shocked that not a single ticket holder had demanded a refund. And to make things worse, I had become the subject of front office discussion.

"Most of the producers have seen his act by now and have passed on it," said Jack Roddy. "The real song, 'Pennies from Heaven,' has had its run, so naturally the parody has no currency anymore. And, face it, Dudley has lost his cutes. He's no longer cute enough or talented enough to sell a song that they have already heard. The novelty is gone. I can't book him."

I overheard all this from the waiting room while Mr. Roddy talked to my dad alone. I guessed they left the door open so I could hear because Mr. Roddy didn't want to look me in the eye and tell me that I was no longer good enough to be in his damned vaudeville wheel.

I was eight years old; my song and dance act was being retired. I was being "red-lighted." Eighty-sixed. Run off. *And* my car was gone!

To his credit, Mr. Roddy later broke the news to me in person. But he took the long way around, looking past me as if I had an evil eye.

"I can always sell a bill with acrobats, jugglers, and a good, clean-talking comic," he said. "But selling novelty acts is always hit-and-miss."

He searched for a child-savvy example. "It's like a teeter-totter. You were up this season, but when you are up, someone else has to be down."

"Like me," I said.

"You got to accept the odds, kid," Roddy continued. "You climb the ladder of your career up a ways, then you slide back down, and then you climb up again, over and over, but you learn to not slide down so far. You've been up a long time, so now you're going to be down for a bit."

His face was fighting with itself. His usually pink nose had little bright red veins showing, and he looked like he was being tugged one way and pulled another. He didn't feel good having to have this talk. I think he must have liked me more than Mother thought.

He ranted on uncomfortably, talking faster and changing his voice on every new thought; he went from embarrassed to quarrelsome. I could smell gin and cigar smoke.

"Big deal! You're young! That's life! You've made some money; you've had your moment. Always remember that when you worked, you *got* your laughs. Not many acts get the laughs you got."

Then he talked himself right out the door of his *own* office. He gave me this parting shot: "We thought you might sing on until your voice changed. No such luck."

I stomped my way back to the hotel, talking out loud about what I *should* have said. I didn't get it. Why was I being tossed off the circuit? How could I go from a big deal to a nothing so fast? What was I? A show-business "has-been" before the age of nine?

At the hotel, Grandmother Riggs gave me a big hug. She was beaming. "Now you get to go to school."

In the 1930s, my folks were playing the big-time vaudeville houses thirty or more weeks a year and easily filled the rest of the year with circus dates. They had their twelve minutes,

37

a well-rehearsed and highly polished hand-balancing act, as well as a second act, a comedy acrobatic act, that worked in theaters and in the circus. They didn't trust the twelve-minute creed. They continued to create new sketches and routines, always adding new acts to their roster.

My parents became well known for a short act that was only meant to cover "stage waits" but became their most popular offering, though the manager treated it as "cherry pie"—a filler act they performed for free. It consisted of a little five-foot-wide stage, like a fabric closet on wheels. The curtains were pulled aside to reveal two little figures, a man and woman with tiny bodies but with my folks' full-sized heads. Doc and Lil called themselves "The Humanettes."

The look of the act was very much in the style of a then-popular newspaper cartoon that featured tiny characters drawn with very large heads. They were presented as "Faces from the Funny Papers." The doll hands were controlled by sticks and the feet were attached to little mallets, so that when they did a tap routine, the little tap-shoed feet would beat back and forth across the stage. This tiny husband and wife sang and danced on a miniature stage, set in "one"—meaning in front of the main curtain. They would be called upon to perform during major scenery changes, and it worked well, with some rehearsed music and a lot of improvisation. The producer expected them to fill the time needed to make the scenery shift—no matter how long it took—performing until the stage manager cued them that the next act was set to go on.

In full makeup, dressed up like a couple on their way to the Easter parade, this miniature marionette couple tapped the dance steps and sang a sweetly sarcastic song directly to the audience, all the while keeping an eye on the stage manager, who would signal if the next act was ready to go on.

Doc: *I wrote a little song the other night*
And put it on the shelf.
(Now are you on? Now are you on?)

Lil: *Now any song that he can sing*
He thinks he wrote himself.
(Now are you on? Now are you on?)

Doc: *Now don't pay any attention to her*
She has an awful gall.
She thinks that she knows everything
When she knows nothing at all.

Lil: *Well . . . how can I know anything?*
When that thing knows it all?
(Now are you on? Now are you on?)

Jack Roddy often bragged, "When there is an accident in the circus, they call out, 'Clowns!' In vaudeville, they call up 'The Humanettes.'" The Humanettes saved many performances by covering these unexpected stage waits, entertaining the audience so that the show could fix itself. Stagehands loved it; it saved their jobs. I, too, loved the act and how new it always seemed, and I'd play in the little stage myself in the wings between shows. After their three minutes of rehearsed song material, everything else had to be created on the spot: holding the crowd, inventing a moment of fun, presenting their "Faces from the Funny Papers" while staying in character and monitoring the crisis backstage. Riggs & Riggs would never have thought of their filler act as being something called "improvisational theater," but that is exactly what it was.

★ 3 ★

THE WORLD'S FAIR

"Are you with it?"

The opening of the New York World's Fair in April 1939 was enormous. Advertisements used phrases like "A Century of Progress" and "A World's Fair to Celebrate the End of the Depression." My father did radio announcements for the fair in which he said, "The World's Fair speaks to all Americans, pointing the way to a new beginning, an America on the threshold of a great tomorrow, an America made whole again through the wonders of science and the power of technology. Every American citizen should see and hear all that the World of Tomorrow predicts for our future, not the future thirty to fifty years ahead, but the future that starts tomorrow, this week, at the New York World's Fair." Because of his radio announcements, Doc became known as the Voice of the Fair.

On opening day, the mayor and other dignitaries joined

President Franklin Delano Roosevelt on the podium. But I "knew" that it was Doc's radio spots that really got people to come to the fair. Doc believed in the fair, just as he believed in what he called "the power of the public, the power of the people in the audience." He enjoyed seeing their faces, enjoyed watching the spring in their step as they came down the ramp after seeing the World of Tomorrow exhibit with its futuristic cars and kitchens. He liked seeing people transformed by the fair's message of hope and prosperity, and he believed in the humanity of what he called the "show-going public." Doc was sold on the fair.

"We are in the business of entertaining that public, that's what we do," he would tell me. "We don't grow corn, or make furniture, or sell insurance. All we can promise is a few laughs, some pleasant memories, and something to talk about tomorrow." The World's Fair offered the perfect job for my dad, something he was proud to promote because he really believed in it.

I was told that every "important" nation built pavilions to present samples of their country's products, politics, and culture, all under the banner of "Peace and Prosperity." Russia, England, Japan, and Italy all had pavilions. Italy spent more than a million dollars on an art deco modern palace celebrating Italian art, food, and an on-time rail system. Famous architects built futuristic structures with newly developed materials that evoked a future not just for America, but also for all the nations of the world. The message of these exhibits was that the future of the world looked bright.

The fair certainly made the future look brighter for our family. The fair provided two seasons of work—thirteen months over two years at top money.

"If this keeps up, we'll all be able to get our teeth fixed!" Jack Roddy quipped.

The first season of the fair bested all expectations for attendance. Billboards proclaimed, "It's getting bigger and better every day. Don't miss the New York World's Fair!"

In the second season the public was happy, some even looking forward to going to the fair a second time to see the new 1940 additions. There was talk of making the fair a permanent year-round attraction. Hoping to make that happen, Mayor LaGuardia or some other political figure was on the fairgrounds every day staging publicity stunts for newsreel cameras.

All the circus and variety acts in the amusement area were expected to do free acts for these photo ops. The Ben and Betty Fox duo did their dance act on top of the Brooklyn Bridge. The Royal Hanneford Circus brought a beautiful Belgian horse to Wall Street for a photo captioned "Investment advice, direct from the horse's mouth." And my father did a handstand on top of the Empire State Building!

When I was eight years old, such events did not seem to be especially out of the ordinary. Using daredevil stunts to draw a crowd had become a popular form of show business advertising. "These free acts are just part of what we do for a living," said Doc when people would ask, "Why? Whatever for? Are you crazy?" Like his father and grandfather before him, Doc was simply dedicated to entertaining the public.

On the way over to the Empire State Building the day of the feat, my mother had quibbled, saying, "You are such a company man, Riggs. Always willing to do free promotion and cherry pie." She was being more than a little sarcastic about his having voluntarily taken the job. I could always tell when she was ticked at my dad; she'd add the word "Riggs" to the end of the sentence.

"If it sells tickets, it helps us. If the fair does well, we all do well." He said it like he meant it. I guess he really was a company man.

Doc and I performed part of The Riggs Family Acrobatic Act in the Sky Lobby, located in the entrance of the Empire State Building's observation deck, under a huge red, white, and blue banner that read "America Is High on the New York World's Fair." A small audience of confused sightseers applauded the unexpected show, then watched as the camera crew set up for Doc's big finish. Everything had to go off exactly as planned if the photographers were going to get the shot they came for. We waited until they got just the right angle of sunlight. Then the photographers, safely belted on a scaffold platform, took pictures of Doc doing a chair handstand on the shoulder of the building, just below the observation deck. The platform allowed them to get bird's-eye pictures of my dad pressing up to a handstand with the other buildings in the background, about eight hundred feet above the street.

My mother was a little edgy, not because of the height but because of the wind. She said it might gust enough to be a problem. She was holding my hand tighter than usual and was looking about, checking for anything that might be out of place. That was the first time in my life that I ever remember thinking that my father could possibly fall. I had seen him do the same handstand on the same chair for as long as I could remember, and we had worked these photo gigs on other buildings a few times before. But *this* was the tallest building in the world.

The breeze was just enough to blow Dad's hair and pants cuffs. One of the newsreel guys said, "The wind blowing his pants really makes the picture." A photo ran in the *Sunday Rotogravure Magazine,* and I heard that the one-minute fair promotion played in newsreel theaters from coast to coast.

In the cab on the way back to Queens, I sat between my folks. They were holding hands and talking sweetly to one another.

One day not long afterward Jack Roddy showed up backstage, looking like he had just come from a wake instead of the front office.

"Bad news. We have a holdback on payday."

"Again?" said Doc. "Pardon me for saying so, but this is lousy timing."

"But it's hitting everybody, the whole country is hurting," said Jack. "Just when we were pulling out of the basement, when everyone was looking ahead to better times, when people were feeling like they might have some little bit of a future."

That was the beginning of a slow slide in morale that lasted all summer. The news abroad was getting everyone disturbed. The fair had lowered the admission price and cut back on salaries. The artists were supporting the enterprise with money earned but not received. Mother stopped looking for that house in Queens. There would not be a permanent World's Fair.

The show kept going on, but the audiences were very tense. In the face of fear, what some thought to be satire was just actors working too hard for laughs that weren't there. By now everyone was resigned to war. No grand tour, no show plans, no artistic breakthroughs could be made without considering war.

In 1940 the Italian Pavilion at the World's Fair was gone, the red carpet was a year older, and the new uniforms that were added to the production numbers were not quite a color match. Still, the gates opened on time every day.

Gypsy Rose Lee's Broadway show *The Streets of Paris* continued to be the big draw, but a new show called *Twenty Thousand Legs under the Sea* was edging her out with cheaper tickets and a woman in a very skimpy wardrobe who danced with an octopus. We were presenting fifteen vaudeville acts, two a day, three a day on weekends. But despite our long rehearsals and artistic efforts, the Parachute Tower amusement ride always had the longest lines.

A "girlie" grind show, doing five shows a day, starring an "old friend" of Doc's, was getting most of the action at our end. Annette Delmar was featured performing a veil dance in front of a painting of Satan. One day, between shows, I got to peek in on the Satan Dance. Miss Delmar was not wearing any clothes at all that I could see.

"Now you know what the attraction is," said my mother. "Attendance always rises in a direct ratio to the visible skin area of the feminine personnel," said Grandmother Riggs.

The year before, the only naked flesh visible at the fair was under water, thanks to Salvador Dalí's exhibit with a glass-enclosed pool framed on one wall. Nude "mermaids" would swim into view, giving ticket buyers a glimpse of a bare breast. This year you could get anatomy lessons all over the grounds.

If the 1939 fair had been a high-class look forward to a bright and happy future, the 1940 version fell back on nostalgia, patriotism, and sex. The ads read: "This year's World's Fair is dedicated to those common Americans, with simple American tastes." Some people had said they stayed away the first year because they thought that they might not understand it or that they might embarrass themselves. They didn't want to be "high-hatted" by those sophisticated artists and highbrow city planner types. Marketing downward worked to get in some bigger crowds, but they spent less money. For a while, business picked up, but it couldn't last.

I was told that closing day set the record for attendance—nearly half a million people had made it out to Flushing Meadows. But although people had lined up for hours to see the World of Tomorrow, they just didn't have enough time or money left once they got to us. Our little vaudeville show was not that big a draw.

"If they don't want to buy your tickets, there's nothing you can do to stop them," the PR guy said. Doc managed to look confident, even when there was nothing coming in; he always acted as if a great amount of work was just around the corner. But for many of the other acts, confidence was in short supply. The backstage noise I overheard ran from grumbling and whimpering to outright agitation.

"This is just a bad location. No wonder we couldn't draw

flies," said Mark, a juggler, one day. "Face it, this is just a rotten show!"

I remember Grandmother slamming down a makeup box. "You must never knock the show. If you are with it, you're for it. If you're not for it, then get away from it!"

Actors will fight with each other, and they'll fight with the director and the playwright, but they do become loyal to the show. After a while they bond with each other to accomplish something onstage and that becomes stronger than everything else. This assumed real importance when we began to work improvisationally in the 1950s. There were a lot of disappointments along the way. Luckily, there were actors willing to hang in there while we developed a new kind of theater . . . and were falling on our face. You had to be "for it" in order to get "it" off the ground.

★ 4 ★

THE RIGGS BROTHERS CIRCUS

Here today, gone tomorrow!

The World's Fair had been such a big deal, and Jack Roddy said all that steady work had got us spoiled. "Now is the time for you to get with it, and find us some new bookings," said my dad.

"I know how much you like good conditions and steady work," Roddy replied, "but for you to get work today, you may have to take some split weeks or do some upping and downing . . ." He paused to make his point. "But at least you'll be working."

Jack was underestimating my dad, who had a bigger goal in mind.

When the producers of the World's Fair settled up with

the performers, they still owed Doc quite a bit of money because he had produced some of the shows. The owners made an offer to my father. They would sign over certain physical assets to cover much of the back salary still owed to us on closing day.

I still have the list of what Dad got out of the settlement:

Flameproofed canvas. Two 120-foot round ends and three 60-foot midsections, making a 300-foot-long circus big top—from O. Henry Tent and Awning Company.

Four 54-foot center poles, bailing rings, stakes, quarter poles, side poles, canvas sidewall, and a complete 40-foot marquee.

1938 REO Speedwagon canvas truck with trailer.

1938 REO semitrailer pole wagon, 72 feet long.

1935 Chevy seat wagon—stringers and jacks with 1 × 12 seat planks.

Approximately 2,100 blue seats.

900 red folding chairs—the reserved section.

One generator.

Four cage wagons, bull truck, cookhouse van, pie car, and other vehicles totaling 25 titled pieces of rolling stock.

The big top was new at the start of the fair; the trucks had only one season on them—or twenty-five thousand miles. No animals were included—all the livestock had left with the acts when the World's Fair ended or had been returned to the World Jungle Compound in Thousand Oaks, California.

In all, there were 110 listed items. My dad now had everything necessary to run a circus—the Riggs Brothers Circus. Not necessary was item number 73.

Number 73 was a bronze casket containing the mummified remains of a male Tasmanian pygmy, which had been widely heralded as the Devil's Child in a special sideshow presentation at the World's Fair. My mother was appalled.

"I have not the slightest interest in being in that kind of show business," she said. Nothing would allow her to think of herself as being anywhere near a sideshow or in any way associated with something called the Devil's Child. She threw a royal snit, condemning the deal. "What are you thinking about, Riggs?"

On first sight, the Devil's Child was startling to see. In life, this tiny man had a well-developed, athletic body, curly red hair, and an expressive face. It looked as if two short stub horns had erupted through his forehead, and he had a tail. His incisors had sharpened points, making his smile all the more menacing. In short, he looked like the Devil—with horns and a tail—actually, two tails. The Devil's Child was presented stark naked, lying on blood-red silk satin inside the bronze casket.

I don't believe Doc really wanted the Devil's Child. It just came with the circus that he acquired from the World's Fair, but for years he was reluctant to get rid of it. As a result, and with space being short on the bus, for years the Devil's Child's casket was stored in a compartment under *my* bed.

At that time, Grandmother Riggs, my parents, and I lived in a sixty-foot luxury motor home for about half the year; the other six months we lived in inexpensive hotels. The motor home, a former Greyhound bus, had been custom-built to our specifications by the Luxury Motor Home Company of Tulsa, Oklahoma. The double-deck bus was modified to create a three-bedroom, two-bath, home on wheels. The living space for three adults and me was tight, but roomier than most of our hotel suites.

At the height of the Riggs Brothers Circus, we had a full, three-ring circus that traveled by truck. It was a big show with more than one hundred trucks and trailers and a three-thousand-seat big top. Doc had a great eye for talent but a weakness for beauty, and a soft heart, so unemployed people kept joining the show, and the show got bigger and better. Other circuses had gone broke, but we stayed on the road, and animal acts with a lot of exotic mouths to feed joined our show just to get stock feed and enjoy the cookhouse. Doc said these acts could work with us until they found something better.

People used to think of the circus coming to town as a big event, and always being new and unique. Circus posters, programs, and announcements love to use a lot of colorful adjectives and alliteration, a tradition started by P. T. Barnum and exploited most effectively by the Ringling Brothers and Barnum & Bailey Circus throughout the twentieth century.

"The circus must bring something new and wonderful, something the public has never experienced before. And it has to do that year in and year out," our manager, Jack Roddy, would say. "An elephant was a real oddity back when Barnum was touring; he had the only elephant on this continent. Now it's hard to find a kid who hasn't seen, petted, or maybe even taken a ride on one."

The circus menagerie brought a zoo of exotic animals to the people all across America at a time when the circus stood alone. The circus was important back then. The old big-top railroad circus made its impact on the country because it went to every major city. But the mud-show circus went to the people in small towns. A new town, a new audience every day. The circus was the only *live* professional entertainment they might experience all year.

Moving a "tented city" was very hard work that required a vast amount of labor, men working eighteen-hour days for little pay. "You have to respect the working men, they move the show," Doc said. He never called them "roustabouts," or "roughnecks," or "razorbacks," as some did. To Doc, they were essential and deserved to be called "the working men."

When you were booked on a show, you might never get to know more than a few names, and the names you did know were ranked by your need to know. I didn't *need* to know the property boy by anything other than Props. Or the electrician by anything beyond Alek. Pie Car John and Gofer and Gilly were named by their jobs. Old Number Seven was the driver of ticket wagon number seven. Lots of men were known only by where they came from, but Tex and Oakie were actually from Nebraska; it didn't matter. There were also guys named Numb Nuts, Sprain Brain, and Killer. I never wanted to know where they came from, only that they could do the jobs they were hired for.

I didn't need anyone's name if I didn't have to talk to them. "We must speak upwardly," Grandmother Riggs taught me. "We only talk downwardly when it involves moving the help." The circus was not a classless society. As a performer, I could speak to the front-office brass, other performers, riggers, and property boys. I was told not to talk to the rest. The canvas crew, trainmen, and the grandstand crew would be finished working by the time I got to the lot. Knowing workers' job names was thought to be enough because the workforce kept changing with new hirings and firings about every week. Those working men who had started the season by giving up half of the first two weeks' pay as a "holdback" could sometimes be counted on to stay all the way back to winter quarters in the fall. But many were like the show itself, "Here today, gone tomorrow."

Circus booking agents used to make contractual arrangements with a town to present the circus and then would rent a vacant lot from the town and get the license. Then the circus came to town. "Circus Day" was a big deal and required a lot of labor. A "punk pusher" was employed to do what we called "pushing punk"—hiring eighth-grade children who would help put up the tent and the seats in exchange for a free ticket to a show. The kids would usually be seated in the cheap seats and might be called out to help during the shutting down, sometimes robbing the kids of the finale. But they could all brag that they had been "with" the circus.

———— •◆• ————

We depended on people showing up and buying tickets at the door. Once when we were in Ohio, the preacher of one town gave a sermon and said it was sinful to go to the circus. We ended up with a small house, and we didn't even have the money to buy enough gasoline to get all of the trucks to the next town. The Phillips 66 truck came in to gas up all the trucks, but we were only able to put one gallon in each truck.

We had to get off the lot the next day or else we would be fined and charged another day's license. We had put just enough gas in the trucks to get them started up and off the lot, and then, one by one, they all ran out of gas along the way to the next town. In the meantime, the advance man went ahead and, luckily, sold an advertising account to a Texaco gas station, which then sent its tanker truck back down the road to gas up our trucks so we could all get into town in time to do the show.

By the third or fourth town after that, when everything was looking really dark, we'd do three full sold-out or "straw" houses—an exceptional kind of run in which all of the seats were sold, and additional people would be allowed to sit on straw on the hippodrome track in front of the rings to watch a slightly shortened show. It was feast or famine. We'd go from sold-out-plus houses to getting only one paid admission, all in a matter of a week. The circus business then was like gambling, but with very few jackpots.

Once, we did a full evening performance when there had been only a single ticket sold. Importantly, the solo ticket had been purchased by an unmarried woman, a school-teacher, who happened to be the daughter of the local sheriff. Everyone else in the audience was either a "punk" kid or people in on free passes. "There's show business and then there's . . . slow business," said Lil. The show went on, and to make it less embarrassing, we moved all the people down in front of the center ring. This record small audience saw a full, two-hour and ten-minute performance for one paid admission. "Small house or SRO—the audience always gets a full performance of the Riggs Circus," said Doc.

> *Whether it's cold, or whether it's hot,*
> *We shall have weather, whether or not!*

So proclaimed our announcer while standing in the center of the center ring. Prince Paul—he was Count Paul another year—was trying to calm an Oklahoma audience's concern, a concern made evident by the quiet murmuring and chattering of the few families that had started moving toward the exits.

"Don't worry, folks, this is just a passing shower," he lied. "The show is not over yet. So please stay in your seats." In the backyard we could hear the announcement, and I knew that this was going to be a night to "John Robinson" the performance. That meant to shorten it, a term named after a famous Civil War–era circus producer.

Our circus performance was only about a third over, so if every act worked its full routine, the audience had nearly one hundred minutes of show coming, and that was too long a time with the dangerous storm that was beginning to pick up some wind. The word was passed—"John Robinson"—at the same time that the canvas crew was rolling out of the sleeper, half-dressed, cursing, and complaining, but lining up around the stake line to pull down the guy lines and tighten the already water-heavy canvas.

"We have a public trust to entertain the audience and get them safely on their way," Doc said in his best dressing-room style. "So let's give them a wonderful performance in less than half the time." Everyone rallied; each act performed its opening and closing routine, heard the ringmaster's whistle, and took a bow.

The audience loved it and were home safely by the time the wind opened *its* act with a double flourish, raising the big top high enough to pull the quarter pole stakes and blowing the menagerie top completely away. I was frantically pulling my flying rigging out into the backyard when I looked up front toward the midway and saw that the banner line, the sideshow, and the menagerie were gone!

"Something's odd," I thought. "They haven't started the tear down yet." But those tents were gone.

Thirty thousand square feet of O. Henry canvas were traveling like a big sail across the highway and over a mile of Oklahoma cornfield. In the big top, the boss canvas man hacked the center pole lines, which allowed the bailing rings to slide down the poles, collapse the balloon of canvas, and saved the big top. Later, as the sky cleared and the rain stopped, the emergency siren on top of the town hall finally started giving out its warning, an hour too late. In the rubble, our Greyhound bus was nowhere in sight. We had lost our home.

"It's a good thing I John Robinsoned the show," said Prince Paul. "At least nobody got hurt!"

The boss canvas man shouted something about getting a friggin' merit badge and then getting the hell away from the poles just as the storm made a parting shot. Lightning struck the flag on the end pole, traveled down the steel cables, and grabbed Prince Paul. There was an awful smell like burned wool and ozone. Doc crouched down low, managed to drag him under a flatbed, where a Red Cross volunteer covered him up with a blanket. Paul was in shock for a while but recovered. A year later, Paul still used his "whether it's cold, or whether it's hot" line, but never with quite the same conviction.

We were tired, and we had lost much to the storm, but we had *not* suffered as much as the towners, where lives had been lost. The sun broke through the clouds as Doc said, "The canvas can be replaced—thank John Robinson and thank Chubb Insurance—we have a show to do in Tulsa." He started making calls to reassemble the Riggs Brothers Circus.

Fortunately, Lil and Grandmother Riggs missed the storm. They had left for Tulsa that morning.

The Oklahoma National Guard found a few pieces of our former home. The frame and the motor had ended up in the middle of a cotton field two miles down the road. Small pieces of the custom plywood cabinets and parts of photo albums and show posters were found in the mud. I found one photo—of Riggs & Riggs: Those Different Acrobats—and wiped the mud away. We still had a circus, but no place to sleep. We were safe, and I knew that we would recover.

Because of the storm, the Riggs family lost not only show

property and equipment, but also the personal belongings from our home. Grandmother Riggs forever grieved over family records, photographs, and show advertisements that were gone, and her beloved china tea service that she had kept intact since her marriage in 1895. Publicity photos, newspaper clippings, and the record of births, deaths, and marriages (which were kept in the otherwise unused family Bible) were gone.

And I began to feel that everything truly was ephemeral, just as Grandmother Riggs had always said. The circus had been wrecked, but I knew Doc would fix it. He mobilized the crew to start unwrapping the wet canvas from around a garage and motel that had been gift-wrapped by the wind.

Our clothing, contracts, show wardrobe, props, and "walk-around" money went with the storm. The American Red Cross provided army cots set up in the East Side High School gym and helped us wire Roddy for money. We were given some dry clothes and a hot meal and told to go to the church for emergency assistance. There was a line of about twenty people passing by a desk where small amounts of cash and some coupons were being handed out. A Salvation Army officer in full uniform cut the two of us out of the herd of the needy. This became a depressing moment.

"Ain't you them show people?"

I nodded.

"We heard about you show people from Reverend Johnson. We can't help you out. You should go to the Church of the Burning Cross over on the east side."

We were strangers, transients, and the word *circus* on the side of our bus had alerted the "protectors" of the village.

These folks had stayed away from the performance. "The storm came to punish the circus," said one woman who would not look at me.

At the Church of the Burning Cross, we were met at the door by none other than Reverend Johnson, who quickly walked us back out of the church and down the cement steps, away from the eyes and ears of the volunteers.

"You are those show people, right?" he asked rhetorically.

We both nodded this time.

"Well, the long and the short of it is, we can't help you out either. All our emergency money comes from the main office, and we can only give it out to local residents."

(We must have riled something in his inner Christian.)

Doc was resigned to the news. "Well, thank you for the thought of it," he said.

As we turned to leave, the good Reverend Johnson said in a half whisper, "You people can't just walk into town as strangers and expect the town to give you a handout."

I was taken off balance. "What? What is this?" Doc nudged me to shut up and move out.

He kept on. "No, you people do not deserve services in this community."

(We did not request help and didn't need the aggravation.)

By then some of the volunteers were coming closer to see what prompted the good Reverend Johnson to raise his voice.

It was an embarrassing situation. I wanted to explain that we were not trying to pull some con game. But a little prairie fire of anger was building up in me and getting snotty.

"Well, Reverend, we were just passing through your formerly

fine little city when the tornado caught us like it caught a lot of your fine citizens," Doc said. "We did not plan to burden you, and we will be on our way just as soon as Western Union can . . ."

Doc was cut off as someone who called himself Holy Brother Bobby came storming out of the church, red-faced, and sputtering, "How dare you come up here for a handout and then get sarcastic with Reverend Johnson here in God's house! How dare you!"

We were definitely not in God's house. In fact, we were on the sidewalk, moving away fast, wondering why the term "circus people" had ignited so much angry noise.

"I'm going to call the sheriff on you," Bobby shouted. "Maybe a night in our jail will make you infidel carpetbaggers civil. Maybe you will learn to fear God." I was nine years old and was startled and struck dumb. We had lost everything, and now we were being threatened with jail.

As it happens, the jail had also blown away.

The next morning, we picked up cash wired for us from Western Union and caught the train. Despite our losses, we recovered enough to reopen two weeks later in Tulsa. As the train pulled out of the station, my dad was singing softly:

From the day you were born, 'til you ride in a hearse,
Things are never so bad, but what they might have been
  worse.

He sat and stared out the window for no more than a few seconds, and then, with a big smile, asked, "What do you suppose happened to the Devil's Child?" We considered that question all the way to Tulsa.

I imagined some time in the future when the Church of the Burning Cross breaks ground to build their new church and unearths the Devil's Child's casket. I think something as durable as the Devil's Child's bronze casket most likely survived the tornado to provide one last laugh at Holy Brother Bobby.

Show people are always suspect. Back when people stayed put, when we brought the entertainment to the people, our arrival in each new town was an exciting time. CIRCUS DAY was a big event. Most of the people greeted us warmly, but there were always some who saw us only as outsiders. The Settled often greet the newcomer with fear, suspicious of newbies, "others," transients, wanderers, feral strangers (who might steal their daughters).

The Other is both celebrated and feared. (He might be an outsider trying to become an insider! Aren't we all?) And the Settled can seem imprisoned in small-town airlessness. Maybe it is part of the American character: we like to watch celebrities and what they do, and then we judge them harshly. In every new town, we were the Other.

People who have no blood ties anywhere, or rather have no blood ties that they can tie to a location, often have trouble explaining: "Where are you from?" "Where are your people from?" You have to overcome the fear that you're going to be judged in order to perform. When you're onstage, everyone applauds. When you're offstage, you're just another kid, except you're *show people.* I carried that judgment for a long time, and it still hurts to remember.

★ 5 ★

SCHOOL ON THE ROAD

"Why is this child not in school?"

In 1941 we settled for a while in Oklahoma and set up a "winter quarters" as a place to repaint and repair the circus—and put me in school. Starting school at the end of the circus season in October always required a mixture of white lies, short con, and sometimes serious negotiation. My mother's task was to convince the school authorities that her young son had "just transferred into the school district, unexpectedly, quite suddenly," and that she was therefore unable to provide any records from the previous school, which was always, it seemed, hundreds of miles away. I had had several tutors over the years, but alas, there were no previous school records. Our sudden arrival at a school around Halloween was explained by some vague reference to "an unfortunate family emergency" and accompanied by promises of hard work and good deportment.

Nothing was mentioned about the fact that I would not complete the school year. I was comforted by that fact. I knew that soon I could leave it all behind and move on to fun things again, such as working in the circus. By June, when the school session would end and my (nonexistent) school records had still not arrived in the mail, I would already be miles away, in the fifth week of the new circus season, playing thirteen shows a week and—sad now to say—not thinking about tests or passing to the next grade.

On the road, of course, I had a tutor, sometimes a qualified teacher, but usually just someone already on the payroll who could double in brass. She would be my teacher, or at least someone with the show who could be *referred* to as my teacher if a local truant officer were to show up backstage and ask, "Why is this child not in school?"

One season, when I was seven, I was without a tutor for a while. My mother had hired a clown named Bubbles Lake to be my teacher, but my dad fired him when he caught Mr. Lake offering me a swig from his gin bottle. I was never sure of Lake's intentions, but Doc was direct: "I know he's a college graduate, and I know he used to teach school, but Bubbles doesn't get to teach my son . . . anything!" Doc had just that moment tossed Bubbles off the second-floor balcony of our hotel. Bubbles bounced off of the lobby sofa and wasn't hurt too badly—just a broken arm and collarbone. Dad tore up his contract, gave him a Greyhound ticket, and that was the last I heard of Bubbles Lake.

Because we were always moving from town to town, my education stayed a hit-and-miss affair. But there *was* a plan, and there was a Riggs family rule: whenever possible, I was to be in school—that is, when it did not conflict with our bookings.

My mother, of course, valued education. She had finished college before she met my father and got swept away in show business. She said she loved show business, and she loved my father, but she knew that if the Riggs family tradition did not continue into the fifth generation, the world would not come to an end.

My father and my mother remained at odds about education. Doc finished high school but never went to college. Lil came out of college into marriage and was always a little irritated that my education was so often put on the back burner. My mother wanted me to have an education, and Doc wanted me to have a career. For her, school was "preparation for life." For Doc, show business *was* life.

The first time I enrolled for an extended period in an actual school, I was nearly ten. My mother and I went to arrange my placement, but her meeting with the school authorities did not go well.

"Without proper papers, Strang School cannot allow some stranger, some unknown kid, whose parents are in '*the show business,*' to enroll in the Strang school system," the principal said. He pronounced the words *the show business* as if those words were an insult and a threat to his civilized community.

Lil gave it another try. She and I dressed conservatively for our meeting with the school superintendent. Mother dropped the name of the Baptist minister and the mayor and even quoted the work of that great educator John Dewey. All in vain.

School had started in September, and it was now November. "You were not here. It's too bad, but maybe next year. *If* you are still around," we were told. "We are not required by law to provide schooling to migrant workers, Indians, or show people. It's all we can do to school our own and the . . . colored! You are nonresidents. You haven't paid taxes here, so why would anyone expect the county to provide schooling for children of show-business transients?" He spat that last word out with distaste.

As we drove back to our newly rented quarters, Mother kept mimicking the man in his dumb cracker voice. "The county is not required, blah, blah, blah . . ." We were laughing. I thought, I'm not going to school this year, either. Was I disappointed or relieved?

Then Mother had a thought.

"Wait a minute, the county is not required, but what about the state and federal government?"

So Lil visited the Five Civilized Tribes Indian School in Strang, Oklahoma, and had a talk with Chief Keys, a wonderfully wise and oil-wealthy Cherokee who was head of the tribal board. He had a secret school he called the "lab school." He decided that the Strang Public School policy was unfair to all minorities—including show people—and that the Five Tribes should set an example of fairness by enrolling any child that had been unfairly denied a chance to attend school. I was the only candidate. So I became a Five Tribes fifth grader.

I didn't know what to expect. Up until then, the closest thing to a classroom that I had seen in a long time was watching a burlesque sketch titled "Teacher's Pet," a short number that featured a seminude teacher and three of her "students," who were baggy pants comics shouting, "Oh, teacher!"

At Five Tribes I was allowed to make up all my missing class grades, all five of them, and was accepted by the other kids even though I could not prove any native lineage. My mother had *implied* that there was some sort of blood connection to the Creek tribe, but it didn't matter. The kids knew the truth: I was "that show-business kid" and was told to stay home on Indian agent inspection day.

Like most white children, I identified Indians with cowboys. Everything I knew about them had come from the movies. I was soon ashamed of this. Chief Keys had saved a lot of kids from being taken away from their families and being sent to an Indian-assimilation boarding school. Keys was a man of peace who said, "I have stayed angry in my head but not in my heart."

At Five Tribes Indian School, I was accepted by the kids after running a single gauntlet. I was fast enough to make it through the line without any loss of blood. When I came back, they dropped their sticks and let out a big yell. No one made fun of my looks, my stupid answers, or my pale face. I learned more than the three Rs. I learned when to look people in the eye, and especially when *not* to look people in the eye. I learned how to be with other kids, but I still thought of myself as an adult.

"School's not so bad," I thought. "I like being around other people, even if they are my own age."

★ 6 ★

THE CIRCUS
AT WAR

When a flyer falls.

1940 had been a very good year. The Depression seemed
over and people once again had jobs and money and hope.
The United States was at peace. The future looked bright, the
circus business was booming.

"It's getting bigger and better every day," said my mother.
"Americans look happy again."

Then came the war.

Soon everything had to be rationed as America mobilized
for war.

And I could see a second war, a war about tradition, education, and values festering between my parents. The Second
World War would cost Doc his marriage, his circus, his health,
and, most tragically, his pride.

———— •◆• ————

"If the Riggs Brothers Circus can't get enough gasoline during the war, we should make the show smaller," Lil said. "The public will understand. The audience will still come to the show."

The war brought a shortage of tires, sugar, and, above all, labor. Everyone was either joining the army or being drafted. The circus had to find ways to reduce the number of working-men and still be able to move the show and get the big top up and down. Like the early railroad, the circus had always required the use of cheap labor—men were hired for their muscle and not much else. Most of the canvas and stake crew were down at the bottom of the pecking order. They fit into the hierarchical caste system below the rest of the workingmen— even below the sometimes hired runaways, winos, and ex-cons. As part of the "top-tier" performing artists, I hardly ever saw any of the workingmen. It's not that I tried not to see; it's just that I didn't.

There was a lot of uncertainty about our future. Every-thing Doc acquired from the World's Fair needed to be re-painted and overhauled if the show was to hit the road again in the spring. The principal painter, a newly unem-ployed scenic artist by the name of Mr. McAdoo, said that he needed six men for four months—"if the circus is to look like a real circus and be ready to open." Mr. McAdoo was a wonderful old man who suffered from a shaking palsy. Even with this affliction, he was able to paint intricate gold leaf lines on the wagons, saying as he painted, "Watch me shake some art off of this paintbrush."

Despite the gasoline rationing, the Riggs Brothers Circus was on the road until Doc closed the show and joined the navy. With the show closing, the animals had to go somewhere. Some went to other circuses, some went to zoos. But more than the whole Noah's Ark of animals, the menagerie of our circus, had to be disposed of before the show could be put to bed. Seats, lights, canvas, and props went into a barn. Seeing Doc's dream circus being taken apart in 1943 made me very sad. We thought that after the war the Riggs Brothers Circus would be resurrected and reopened, but it never opened again.

"I'm going to win the war!" Doc wrote to Lil. "Then I'll be able to buy gas and rubber for the show and continue our scheduled circus tour."

When he had tried to enlist in 1942, the army wouldn't take him, saying he was too old, but in 1943 with the war going badly, the navy made him a petty officer.

1943 was a very bad year. People were frightened and sad. Everyone thought we were losing the war. We got a telegram: Uncle Art was declared missing, shot down over Germany; Father was in the Pacific; my grandmother died, and no one told me. (This still hurts.)

With the strain of these terrible times, my parents divorced. The Riggs Brothers Circus folded the big top forever. I did my part, too, by getting sick, spending nearly a year at the Mayo Clinic fighting nephritis. I got well, obviously, but by that time America was winning the war, my uncle was liberated from Stalag 17,* my mother had remarried, and I started school again.

After VE Day, my father's navy ship had sat on the equator for eight weeks while they were waiting for the troops to arrive from Europe. All the men on his ship were sure of their death in the upcoming invasion of Japan, and having by then survived eleven initial landings and losing many of their buddies, they were feeling fatalistic. At that point, men on the ship started tattooing one another, singing some old navy song: "without a sigh, for tomorrow we die."

My father was a navy beach lander. His job was to get marines from the troop ships into the landing boats and then onto the enemy beach. Once a ship's ramp was dropped, the marines went ashore. Doc had only to run fifty paces from the landing craft, dig in, guard the craft, and await a return trip with the casualties. Those first fifty steps often took the heaviest enemy fire. Of the 350 beach landers who trained with my dad back in Oakland, only twelve came back alive.

When he came back from the war, his body was covered with tattoos. "I'm a moving picture show," he said. His charming cheerfulness was replaced with a hair-trigger anger. "They say I'm Asiatic now," he said, using a slang term for the "battle fatigue" that came between World War I's "shell shock" and post-traumatic stress disorder in more recent wars.

---

* Arthur Riggs was a prisoner of the Germans for fourteen months in a prisoner-of-war camp that just so happened to be called Stalag 17.

Before the war, we had standards: every Riggs act was rehearsed, polished, and re-rehearsed "to be the very best." The war had changed Father. He was no longer eager to rehearse. Now he was willing to settle for second best. Tears welled up in his eyes when he explained: "We are a variety act, we are only one part of a variety show, we are not headliners anymore. Our act fills out the evening's performances between the star acts. There is no onus on the Riggs reputation because we will be very good at being good enough." That was a tragic change.

In 1947, when I was fifteen, we started getting a lot of engagement offers from overseas. We took our act out of the country, thinking we were hot stuff. In London we were the "imported act, direct from the USA," deserving of better billing because we were new to the British.

I learned a new lesson about tolerance. The homegrown English acts were gracious and revealed none of the resentment that American acts often felt about jobs being filled by those "hooligan" foreign acts. There was much less jealousy in the British circus, or maybe they were just better at concealing it behind English reserve. At any rate, we were treated to good conditions; we were respected and paid very well, and I tried to live up to my billing without becoming impossibly temperamental. I tried.

I was billed as "The Great Alberty." It was a big surprise. I thought I was pretty good, but I had never thought that I was great.

Our contract clearly had us booked as The Flying Riggs

Brothers; my pole act was just an extra act we offered along with the clowning back when we were exchanging telegrams. Now we were in England ready to perform two acts in the show, and management expected three.

When we arrived for the first rehearsal, I was surprised to find that someone named Clive had given me a brand-new stage name and a separate identity on the program. The circus producer in London just decided that The Great Alberty would be the best name to give the American kid who had been hired for the holiday production. I was told the programs and posters had been printed, it was too late to make changes, and I was expected to *become* The Great Alberty. I had never wanted to be anyone other than a Riggs, so I was a ticked-off teenager.

"You will do the act as you always do," said the director. "The only change will be the announcement." He smiled and gave me a little salute, saying, "Mister Alberty."

I went through some ego swallowing, but by dinnertime I had talked myself into liking the name. I carried on a debate in my head. I thought, "Alberty could conceivably be construed as honoring my uncle Al, and at least they didn't give me some name that's hard to say like Ugo Dematsiatsy. And Alberty is first alphabetically. It should be easy for the fans to remember, and it *is* the center ring."

I must have said center ring out loud because Doc spoke up: "There is *only* the center ring here; in England, every act is center ring." Doc went on to explain the publicity snafu. It turned out to be a vagary of deadlines. "Clive said he couldn't reach us while we were on the ship, so he went with the first name he could think of to make his printing deadline. You always said you'd like to have a job that didn't depend on the Riggs family name. Well, Son, you got it!"

He was putting me in my place and complimenting me at the same time. At least that's what I thought. "'Great' is a word for the towners; 'great' is to sell tickets. I'm not sure it will mean much to the British. They have never been an easy sell. Just don't go getting temperamental on us," I was told.

The poster was only a "two-sheet," small by bill-posting standards, but it had my new aerial stage name in big block letters. (The war was over, but paper was still being rationed, as was damn near everything.) It read, "Spectacular Sway Pole Sensation: The Great Alberty." I started swaggering a little, feeling much more important than I could ever be. Doc caught me as I was bulling my way across the ring. "Don't get too cocky," he said. "We're getting the same salary as before."

In the holiday presentation of the Blackpool Tower Circus, my third-from-closing spot on the program was introduced with a trumpet fanfare and this announcement:

"Absolutely awesome acrobatics, amazingly achieved
at an astonishing altitude by an accomplished
agile aerial artist, the king of the air!"

The announcer would pause, as the drum roll grew louder, and end with: "The Great Al-Bert-Tee!" How was I supposed to hear that twice a day and not let it go to my head?

This grandiose, alliterative, redundant style was also used for our bar act earlier in the show. "Hair-raising, heart-stopping heroics by the death-defying daredevil duo: The Flying Riggs Brothers!"

This kind of puffery gave the newspaper critics an easy angle for their columns. If they wanted to potshot any of the acts, the excesses of our intro gave them a license. I felt like we had been set up to draw fire away from the rest of the show. All of the British acts were given straightforward announcements. Maybe management just wanted to prop up the Americans' announcement to an audience that was not totally sold on all things American. It could have been what they thought *we* wanted. Always skeptical, I believed that it was some kind of private joke by the management.

The billing had some other effect on me, however. I had carried a secret, silent hurt around for several years. Mr. Davenport, the circus boss, had once said, "You got hired by Dailey Brothers Circus only because of the Riggs name and reputation. Otherwise, I wouldn't have been interested. Without your dad's name, you are just another nobody." That bothered me a lot, but after a season of work as The Great Alberty, I knew I could make it on what I had to offer. Partly, it was father–son pride, and I had won, even though there had never been a fight. It was all in my head. There was no scene, no "today you are a man" moment. I had done well, and my dad said, "Good job, Son." Having proven to myself and Doc that I didn't *need* the Riggs name, I went comfortably back to being one of The Riggs Brothers.

We got great notices, and the producer splurged with a huge bonus when we closed. The tour was a big success.

A year later I heard that there had been another act billed

as The Great Alberty. I found out he'd canceled the year before, leaving a great supply of posters. The producer, happy to use up the old posters, had dubbed me "The Great Alberty." So much for pride.

1948. I was nearly seventeen, flying well, and getting stronger with every engagement. I was in love with the feeling of vitality, the feel-good exhilaration, the joy of flying. We were booked to do aerial bars and a flying return act. Doc hired a new catcher.

When we played the Boston Garden, I got a profound education in humility, humanity, and the danger of hubris in show business. The building was one of those tall, high-balcony jobs, made for sports, with big accessible girders easy to tie off to and hang the rigging. The floor plates were, however, all too far out, making for net guy wires that were much too loose. We knew we would have to find a fix before showtime. That had to wait because Denny, my new catcher, wanted to get in some of what he called "beer time."

I never got invited along when Denny and P. J. went out drinking because I was still underage. We had hit the city on an odd date, with the setup on a Thursday because of some sports playoff that had, to my dismay, higher priority than the circus. We were to play a split week, making the hall available halfway through the run. The hiring committee—some charity or Shrine club that took the hall on a "days available contract"—had created a lot of extra work for us. On Friday we did an early kiddies' matinee and the regular two shows, tied off all the guy lines, and liberated the space for the basketball game. After all the doubled-up work, we got to take Saturday off. I listened to the basketball game in the dressing room, because the ushers wouldn't let me in without a ticket.

At that time Boston had some kind of Sunday blue laws regarding the sale of alcohol, so Denny's Sunday search for his "morning bump" had been futile. He was in a bad mood, but then he was never in a good mood, so I didn't give it much thought. Denny, half Irish and half Sioux, was a big man and heavier than most catchers. His 250 pounds looked good in the air but had a lot of belly on the ground. He was tough enough and strong enough to bounce me off his chest and make *me* look graceful. I was a pretty good bar performer; my long legs gave my giant swings the advantage of a longer pendulum, but I was constantly reminded that I had grown too tall to ever become a really great flyer.

Never inclined to pay attention to logic, The Riggs Brothers had gone right ahead and offered the flying trapeze act along with the aerial bar act, the juggling act, and the clown numbers, so as to have something to sell. We were actually offering the only non-Hispanic flying act anyone had seen for a long time, with a couple of principal flyers who were too old, a comic leaper who was too tall, and a catcher with a drinking problem.

The band played the "Dream Lover's Waltz," and Doc did the first two fly-outs, out and back, warming up, testing the swing. Then Denny dropped down, swung his legs around the outside of his lines, and wrapped his legs in a Dutch Lock. I heard him groan slightly on the top of his backswing. Doc gave me a quizzical look, as if to say, "What's up with Denny?" I didn't pick up any meaning from the look, so I left the board when Denny topped the front end of his swing, went down the hill, did some comedic bicycle kicks on the backswing for the audience, and passed Denny at the top of the swing. Doc called to me in a singsong voice, "He's-not-high-enough." I could have gone back to the board and started all over, but I was pumped, ready to fly. Pride shaded my judgment.

Freddy Valentine had always insisted, "It's not speed you want, it's height. You have to have height to do the trick and meet the catcher. Height gives you more time before you meet."

In rehearsal, Denny was always forcefully energetic. Now he was moving like mud. I put a lot of kick in my swing, as if more energy from me would make up for Denny's flaccid arc. I came down the "hill," popped as high as I could, reached for his wrists . . . and found only air. My rotation continued, and my feet came up and connected with Denny's head, making a very soft thud sound. My rotation stopped. I fell, eyes to the sky, flat as a board, out of control, into the net below. Denny, nearly unconscious, swung his legs together, fell out of his lock, and dropped like a slab of cement.

My first bounce into the net had lifted the crow's foot off its pin, and it sagged in toward the center pole. At the bottom of my second bounce, Denny landed on top of me, and the whole center of the net collapsed into the sawdust. I heard the band switch to clown music, with people yelling, and the sound of the whistle. I couldn't move. I thought Denny must be dead. Then he cursed and rolled off me and slowly went from hands and knees to both feet and staggered out of my sight. I don't remember anything after that.

I woke up the next day in a Boston hospital, in a body cast, and feeling a lot of pain. I had a broken collarbone and left arm, and my ribs had been pulled away from the sternum. My right side had been spared, except for a broken pinky finger. The doctor said I had been in shock, but that my head was okay, and that my big body cast would be replaced after a few days. I knew "from tradition" that the show would go on without me.

I was told that when we came crashing down the ringmaster called for "Clowns!," then "Bulls!," and reordered the lineup, bringing the elephants in on the hippodrome track for the always popular long mount. This refocused the crowd, blocked their view of the ring, and allowed for a graceful finale to the show. He closed the performance announcing happily that everyone was alive, safe and sound, and imploring, "May all your days be circus days!"

The announcer had kept the audience happy and had kept the lid on the story so as not to spook future attendees. "Circus accidents make for very bad press and knock the hell out of the box office," said the boss. The story made the local newspapers, a single column three inches long. I was nearly killed and couldn't even make the front page.

The engagement ended, and the show moved on to Chicago along with my father, who was under contract—leaving me stranded in the hospital in my hot, itchy body cast. I was angry and childishly looking for someone to blame. Denny was at the top of the list, as was my own lack of judgment. Denny worked the rest of the engagements. The show must go on.

When a flyer falls, you go to the hospital, but the show goes on.

★ 7 ★

FLYING FUNNY

"Absolutely awesome acrobatics, amazingly achieved
at an astonishing altitude by an accomplished agile
aerial artist, the king of the air!"
How was I supposed to hear that twice
a day and not let it go to my head?

I had never had a five-year plan, always needing to keep things open in order to be available for work, but I knew it was time to grow up and do a little life planning. I had always been in the family act, always on a team, always saying "we" instead of "I." It was time for me to get out on my own. Doc was now putting everything into producing clown numbers, and he wasn't very interested in my idea for a circus act with original music and a fantasy story to tell.

"The Riggs tradition is what counts," he said. "They don't want to hire us to do some kind of 'avant-garde' aerial act. Save your money; they don't want new music." It was time for me to do new things.

Dubb Harden, my onetime rigger, had a short season that ended in New Jersey, so he hopped on the train and came to see me. He had a lead on a sway pole rigging that he said I could pick up for five bills, but when I saw some pictures of it, I felt chills. It was sleek and well painted but poorly engineered.

"Why is this rig for sale?" I asked. There had been a number of aerial accidents recently, and I had for some weird reason been keeping track. Some circus people had been coming crashing down because of faulty equipment, almost always because of some kind of rigging failure.

"I think it's part of an estate sale," said Dubb, who didn't know much.

"Oh, damn, do you think?"

"Pipe broke," he said.

"Pipe? Do you mean a pipe, like as in gas pipe, with a seam?"

"I think he tried to make do with two-inch electrical conduit."

I told Dubb to keep looking.

After I was discharged from the hospital I caught up with the show on closing day in Atlanta and started working my body back into shape. Everything had healed, and I was beginning to get a full range of motion, but I was weak from bed rest and could hardly lift my own weight. With The Riggs Flyers no longer available for bookings, I was out of a job. I started working out long days, eating big steaks, and pushing myself back into a flying condition.

"How would you like to be a catcher in an unnamed famous flying trapeze act?" I asked Dubb. Six weeks later we

were doing simple picture tricks, simple "pose and then connect" moves like "skin the cat," and I was getting over being
sore all the time. By spring we had one-half of an act. I had
managed to remount long enough to know that the fall had
not robbed me of anything but time. The feel of flying was still
there. I could still have fun in the air. But first I had to finish
high school.

Most of the old vaudeville and circus acts were set—polished
but never changed or added to. The Riggs family kept adding
more acts to the roster. Everyone seemed to agree that the
most beautiful aerial act was the flying return act, but it was
not the most difficult. John Ringling once said, "The two
hardest acts in the circus are the horizontal bars and Roman
Rings," so naturally Doc insisted on doing both. I came late,
so I missed out on doing the Roman Rings, but the horizontal
bar act was as hard as anything I had ever tried. "Why do we
keep selecting the hardest job?" I asked. "Oh, it's just a family
tradition," said Doc with a smile.

To connect with the audience, we would always "sell" to a
specific spot in the house, a corner in the audience—looking
for a friendly face. On the first bow, we'd find someone in
the audience to make eye contact with and then work to
that someone. In the flying act on the back turn, we would
stomp lightly on the landing and "style" to the young lady over
there, sell it to another group over *here,* try to see how they're
taking it. You hope you have their undivided attention.
The worst thing that can happen is that you make the extra
effort to sell to a certain person, then realize that she is look-

ing somewhere else—watching the balloon salesman go by. (In Europe, the circus in those days never compromised the art by selling merchandise in the big top.)

It was harder to make audience contact in the big halls, where we were farther away from the audience. The big three-ring circus system was, of course, built on greed, as a bigger tent would accommodate a larger audience. It became artistically frustrating when we were working in the number one ring and couldn't see what was going on down in ring number three. Some shows would actually move an act from one ring and play it later in the show in another ring. That was the reason I liked the flying act, because it was usually the only act working at one time. You were high up, and you had all of the audience's attention.

When Doc and I did the ground version of the horizontal bar act (a difficult comedy act, punctuated by straight tricks or dangerous moves), we would work in the program against acts in both end rings, a three-ring display of acts working at the same time. Here we got a humbling lesson. Once when we thought we were doing something wonderful, we styled for the audience. But the audience wasn't watching us. They gave no applause, because they were watching the guy over *there* in ring number two.

That's when we realized that we had not interested *that* audience *that* night, despite the difficulty of what we were doing.

"Everything in show business is either interesting or it's not interesting," Doc said. It was an irony that I did not understand until much later.

In the horizontal bar act I left the bar at the bottom of a giant swing, did a half twist and a half somersault, and landed in a handstand on top of the other bar ten feet away from there. I then continued the circle. When we got really good at this, Doc and I would do what we called "chasing flyovers," passing each other in the center making continual circles of giant swings. It was a risky proposition; a collision could wreck us both. If I underturned the trick, I would cross over and, instead of catching with my hands, I'd slam into the bar with my sternum and most likely tear my ribs. The act was designed to be both a straight and a comedy act, ideal for circus or for nightclubs; it kept me on guard—and with my ribs taped up all year.

We built a low apparatus that had two horizontal bars eight feet high and ten feet apart, a tall mechanism that rolled in and out like a big rollaway bed. We could set up on a little nightclub dance floor, put down weights to stabilize it, and then do the act. For comedic purposes, we'd prepare the safety pads underneath the bars for a surprise gag. I'd sprinkle some talcum powder around the edge of the pad and put another pad on top of that.

The act started with me seated casually in a chair with my feet against the rigging. The audience would see me reading a book titled in big letters: *How to Be an Acrobat.* Doc would enter and complete a demanding routine of giant swings, ending with a somersault, all while I would be sitting there reading the book. Finally, inspired by Doc's example, I would decide to try my luck. I would start to follow the instructions in pantomime, come back, look at the bar, reread the lesson, and finally get brave, jump up, and do a half swing. Just when I reached horizontal, I would let go and fall flat on my back and hit the pad, which would raise a cloud of talcum dust. I then lay there motionless, appearing to be knocked out. The audience would wonder if I were dead. I'd wait a count of ten, then get up like Lazarus in a surprise recovery, go get the book, and tear out the offending page and crumple it up and throw it away.

This ninety-second gag took a fair amount of rehearsal. The comedy came from what the philosophers called "failure exposed and amplified." Every time I would try to do something, I would fail, and then Doc would successfully do something even more spectacular that would challenge me, and then, like Sisyphus, I would try to do the same trick and fail again. Of course, at the end, I'd master the moves—for the big finish. Success at last!

One of the next new things I considered was buying a cannon, a story for another day. It ultimately fell apart, and Mother said, "Go back to school."

I was nearly twenty years old when I finally enrolled in what was then called the Normal School, a teachers' college in the middle of rural Minnesota. I had just returned from a very successful circus tour of Hong Kong, Manila, Hawaii, and Japan. That was after a not unsuccessful European circus tour. I had a little money and was feeling rather full of myself. My age, parlance, Italian clothes, and foreign car made it difficult to blend in. With no local family, no social connections, no record of athletic or scholastic achievement, it was not surprising that someone would ask, "Why did you choose *this* school?"

I enrolled at Mankato State Teachers College (MSTC) because I had no bookings.

I had transported a very bright young lady friend two hundred miles to her dormitory and was about to leave when she said, "As long as you're here, why don't see if they'll let you register? You always said you wanted to go to college someday, so why not here? Why not now?"

I knew it was customary for bright students to start planning for college in junior high school. I missed the planning when I missed junior high. Amazingly, I was accepted. This should not be held against MSTC, which was and still is a fine institution (now Minnesota State University, Mankato).

Joining the other first-year students, I stood out. I soon learned that standing out goes against a well-established Minnesota custom.

My roommate, a business major as well as an accomplished jazz pianist, began the process of orienting me to college life. Chuck McKinsey was a year ahead, so he knew and taught me the ropes. He also introduced me to modern jazz. After years of flying to Strauss waltzes and circus marches, modern jazz was a revelation. Jazz has covertly inspired most of my theatrical work ever since.

We all read the book *How to Think Up* (McGraw-Hill, 1942) in which Alex F. Osborn, a founder of the advertising agency BBDO, introduced the term "brainstorming" to the world. We spent hours discussing existentialism, German theater, T. S. Eliot, and especially the Freudian idea of free association. Trying to impress my tiny group of friends, I said in a delusion of grandeur that I thought that a group of intelligent, talented people, placed in a state of free speech, where all voices and ideas were welcomed, could use free association to create stage entertainment without the benefit of a written script. No one agreed. But everyone had a free-association story. And told it. My idea about applying the technique to theater got lost. The discussion went on and on. Beer was illegally consumed. Friends turned hostile and challenged my un-American idea.

I wanted approval about my theory from peers, but I went about it in the most stupid of ways, speaking with too much assumed authority. I was a new nobody who hadn't taken time to make friends. So I stopped talking about it.

I counseled myself: When you are ready and truly off the road, you can do a degree program. But for now, take the courses that interest you, but be sure to do the work.

I did the class work, but then "real work," offering real money, resurfaced.

CLOWN
DIPLOMACY

My handshake nearly destroyed the circus.

I was just getting acclimated to life in a college dorm in Minnesota when I got a telegram from E. K. Fernandez that changed everything. I could finish the term, but I had to be in San Francisco two days before the start of spring quarter.

The U.S. government had decided that something so American as the circus would help sell the new democratic way of life to the Japanese and build goodwill. It would help heal the wounds of a formerly proud, now defeated people.

E. K. Fernandez was the greatest producer I ever knew. He opened up the entire Pacific Rim to American show business. Fernandez liked "firsts." He was the first to produce the Ice Capades in Tahiti, where they had never even *seen* ice or thought of people skating on it. He moved an entire coral reef to the World's Fair, where it was presented as the "Singing

Sands of Maui." Now he was the first to bring an American circus to Japan after we destroyed Nagasaki and Hiroshima.

"I need clowns, funny clowns," Fernandez wrote. "The Japanese people need to laugh. I'll buy your bar act, but what I have to have is a producing clown who can deliver. Wire me your availability."

As producing clowns, it was our job to devise short sketches and walk-around gags that could live up to E. K.'s challenge. First we would hire a few "wild and crazy guys" who would arrive, hopefully, with an established clown character of their own creation. Ideally, they'd have their own makeup and wardrobe and be able to "think funny." It's amazing how many would-be clowns think that the clothes make the man and that all they have to do is *look* funny. Funny is as funny does. Some clowns just look funny; real clowns *do* funny. It's like the difference between saying a funny line and saying a line funny.

For any clown gag to work, it has to be simple and accessible. People need to understand the context and have some empathy for the pain of others. Slapstick comedy can get pretty rough.

If it's funny, someone is feeling pain. When we see someone fall down, our instinct is to laugh. If the person who falls on the ice doesn't get up, *then* it's tragedy. Slapstick comedy works everywhere in the world; the characters change, but a sight gag always gets a laugh. Admittedly, the younger the audience, the easier the laugh.

The only opportunity we really had to spend time up close with the audience was during the "come in" when it was possible to improvise with ticket holders as they *came in* to take their seats. As Alfonso the Honking Pedestrian, I made a point of never speaking words. I greeted newly arrived folks and showed them to their seats, making conversation with them through the use of the several horns and bells I had hidden in my bearskin coat. This allowed me to express some variable emotions, simply with the different sounds. The audience could observe the moment and fill in the blanks with their own thoughts—the "recognition light bulb" would go off and cause them to laugh. All of this preshow entertainment served as a warm-up to the start of the Grand Opening Parade and the show itself.

A lot of our vaudeville acts could cross over to the circus ring by making the movements and the props bigger. When we played as The Crazy Carpenters in vaudeville, the opening would find us at a construction site, hammering and sawing, moving long pieces of lumber and tall ladders about the stage, creating a big Rube Goldberg–kind of puzzle. The audience could see that something was being built despite the many accidental tumbles and pratfalls, and they could anticipate the catastrophe that just had to occur. This was what was called a crazy house comedy acrobatic act with lots of tumbling in and out of windows, leaps through revolving doors, and near-miss collisions. In the end, the whole house came crashing down onstage. We would perform the same acrobatic moves in the circus, but there we became The Crazy House Painters, which allowed for splashing a lot of water-based paint on each other and a small amount of clean water on some audience members.

I suppose what's really funny is that the circus paid us to do all this nonsense. And now we were going to be paid to go to Japan to entertain people who had just lost World War II.

There seemed to be no reason not to take the job, so Doc and I joined the Fernandez company in San Francisco and flew Pan Am to Japan with a couple of refueling stops along the way.

"I can't tell you how important this tour is," E. K. kept saying. "The occupation will end soon, and we must be a credit to the American way of life. They can't just like us; I want them to love us. If this engagement goes well, we might be able to take the show on to Manila and Hong Kong and just keep going west around the world for a couple of years, until we play England and come back to the States a big success and play New York."

This wonderful old man had a dream, and I was ready to hop on for the ride. It was the patriotic thing to do. And it looked like two years of steady work.

Walter Mahatta was the bilingual company manager. A Japanese-American, no-nonsense road boss who always seemed mad about something, he got off on the wrong foot with Doc by making a crack at Doc's expense.

"Doc Riggs only *looks* like Clark Gable at night; in the morning he's just a hobo clown," Mahatta said. Lucky for him, Doc let it pass.

"He doesn't know anything about me, so I'll wait awhile," Doc said. "Maybe I won't have to *educate* him."

In the circus, there was always a lot of "hurry up and wait."

The show's equipment came by ship, and even though it had a three-week head start, it did not arrive until the night before opening. We had to do an all-nighter getting the show hung, so everyone was dead tired the morning we opened. With no time to rehearse, the first matinee (9 a.m.) was a tragedy of errors. There were only two accidents at the opening, but because show people believe that "accidents run in threes," we were all edgy—fearful that the third (other shoe) might drop at any time.

Right off the bat, the second number in the show, Frank Phillips's arena cat act, had flash bulbs popping as Japanese cameramen, hired for opening publicity, triggered an event that gave them a news photo. The American mountain lions freaked from the flashes and started slashing Frank's shirt and chest to shreds. Pumas or mountain lions tend to gang up when there is trouble. African lions will do a sideways slap at the trainer, but pumas do quick, vertical slashes. Blood was flying through the air, the photo guys kept shooting, and the flashes made things worse. Cage boys distracted the other cats and opened the gate, allowing them an exit to the comfort of their cages. Frank managed to beat the lead cat aside, and the whole gang of cats opted for the safety of the chute, and things calmed down. The band had not missed a beat while Frank was fighting for his life. The ringmaster whistled, the band played a D'A' (a circus band two-note trumpet used to punch up a concluding act), and I entered the number two ring to "Galloping Comedians" played heavily on trumpet as Frank limped toward the back door, bleeding from multiple slashes on his face and arms. The steel arena was removed

Featuring
RIGGS & RIGGS
Those Different
Acrobats

*A promotional photograph for my parents' act, taken
a few years before I was born. This photograph was rescued
from the mud after a tornado took our home.*

*A true child of the circus, I perched in the
mouth of a tuba in the spring of 1932.*

*My debut "act" with the Russell Brothers Circus
was as the Polar Prince of the North. The miniature
horse was soon replaced with a polar bear cub.*

LEFT: *I grew up watching my parents perform, and learning from them.*

BELOW: *Playing "Buck Riggs the All-American Cowboy" alongside my father, "The King of the Kokemos," during the circus off-season in 1937.*

Riggs and Riggs

Sensational Comedy Jugglers and
Horizontal Bar Performers
Featuring a Variety of Spectacular Tricks
for Fairs, Night Clubs and Indoor Circuses

NOTE: This is positively the
only Trampolene Horizontal
Bar Act in the U. S. A. at the
Present Time.

We Have These Dates Open

Booking Address
Hand's Park, Fairmont, Minnesota

Riggs & Riggs holiday card, showing my juggling mirror act.

*I'm on the bars practicing my act. Note the
clown shoes (my feet are not that big).*

Taking a break with fellow performer Baba Dewyne in Manila, 1952.

TOP LEFT: *The E. K. Fernandez All-American Circus. I'm ringside at bottom left, holding my hat in the air.*

BOTTOM LEFT: *Opening Day of the All-American Circus. I am spotting my dad on the bars, with Punch Jacobs at right.*

*My controversial handshake with Crown Prince Akihito of Japan,
which caused an international crisis and changed Japanese policy.*

Dudley dangling from the trapeze in the early 1950s.

LEFT: *Performers spend a lot of time waiting in between our shows.*

BELOW: *Entertaining children in a military hospital at Clark Air Base in Manila, 1952.*

Program for the Kelly & Miller Bros. Circus.

AL G. KELLY & MILLER BROS. 2ND LARGEST CIRCUS

OFFICIAL ROUTE

Season 1956   **Card Number 24**

DAY	DATE		CITY		MILEAGE
			Twenty-Fourth Week		
Sun.	Sept.	30	Lake Village,	Arkansas	60
Mon.	Oct.	1	McGehee,	Arkansas	24
Tues.	Oct.	2	Lake Providence,	Louisiana	48
Wed.	Oct.	3	Tallulah,	Louisiana	28
Thur.	Oct.	4	Rayville,	Louisiana	37
Fri.	Oct.	5	Winnsboro,	Louisiana	25
Sat.	Oct.	6	Ferriday,	Louisiana	42
			Twenty-Fifth Week		
Sun.	Oct.	7	Jena,	Louisiana	42
Mon.	Oct.	8	Coushatta,	Louisiana	84
Tues.	Oct.	9	Colfax,	Louisiana	55
Wed.	Oct.	10	Oakdale,	Louisiana	63
Thur.	Oct.	11	Marksville,	Louisiana	61
Fri.	Oct.	12	Abbeville,	Louisiana	97
Sat.	Oct.	13	Franklin,	Louisiana	41

Total Mileage to Date 7480

SID A. STEVENSON, MAIL AGENT

LEFT: *Every few weeks you would receive a new official route card informing you where you were off to next. Note that we visited a new town every day.*

BELOW: *On the road with the Dolly Jacobs Circus along the Alcan Highway—the crowds were not huge.*

My first trip to Minnesota with the Shrine Circus in 1952.
People told me I wouldn't be able to winter tour Minnesota
and the Midwest in my MG, but after a big snow the MG was
always the first one off the lot (but it was "breezy at best").

The New Ideas Program in Minneapolis, 1958.

RIGHT: *Performing with the Instant Theater Company in 1956.*

BELOW: *First promotional shot for Café Espresso in 1959: drinking espresso while doing a one-arm handstand. Photograph by Jim MacRostie.*

RIGHT: *Posing with the first espresso machine in the Midwest, 1956. Photograph by Dwight Miller.*

BELOW: *Always new, always brave. Early days at the Brave New Workshop, 1963. Poster by Richard Guindon. Photograph by Henri Dauman /* Life *magazine.*

from the circus ring to clear the stage for the next act while The Riggs Brothers frolicked on the horizontal bars. Now the audience was laughing, having forgotten the bloodshed (while Frank was being treated by medics). Funny clowns were there to entertain and distract the audience from the reality they had just experienced.

In Japan, we set up in what had been a wrestling arena, a very tall building with forty-five thousand places on the floor to sit. The people in the audience watched the show sitting on their knees on mats. There were a few dozen chairs available to U.S. servicemen and diplomats in a small, closed-in area in front of the center ring, which I, not too wisely, decided to refer to as the royal box. The show had a full brass band, three elephants, a tiger act, *and* an American mountain lion act. There were jugglers, acrobats, Fred Valentine's Flying Trapeze Act, and us—The Riggs Brothers and our "jolly collection of frolicking fools." We had the usual collection of clown wannabes and a couple of workingmen who had been recruited from the props department, well-meaning but short on professional experience. The one truly brilliant clown was a young hobo character named Punch Jacobs.

After just a one-hour rehearsal, the crew learned the acts, including a clown baseball game that we were certain would be a hit, because baseball was so popular in Japan.

The baseball act involved keeping your eye on the ball—but there was no ball. The ball appeared only as suggestion. The pitcher went through all of his motions—windup, a stretch, and an exaggerated throw. There was a moment's pause, and the catcher slapped his glove, raising a puff of dust. The umpire called out "Strike one!" and the game went on. The audience, knowing the rhythm of the game and how the movements were normally paced, soon accepted the fact that there was no ball. In the United States, this pantomime baseball game had always been a big hit with the audience; in Japan, much to our surprise, it died.

"What happened?" stormed Mahatta. "How did you guys make that the most unfunny clown gag in the history of the circus?"

He paused, trying to catch his breath, then walked right up to me and shook his finger in my face. He was standing on tiptoe on the front edge of my clown shoes, looking up, trying to get something else out, but all that came was a gibberish of words, a frustrated mix of Japanese and English. Then he walked away muttering in very loud English something about needing new clowns. Everyone was exhausted, and we had two more shows to perform before we could rest.

The next performance was also a disaster. Nothing happened the way it was planned. The music was off, the pickup musicians hadn't learned the music, the local prop boys wouldn't move until the orders were given a second time in Japanese. They stood and posed in their new uniforms, forgetting what they were there to do. Having just been trounced by the unexpected audience apathy, I asked myself, "Just what *is it* that I am supposed to be doing here, so far from America? What is my job? Do I still have a job?"

I was sure that Mahatta was making a list of people to fire. If this performance got bad press, someone would have to be blamed.

We ended with a spirited, patriotic flag finish. The audience for the second show was lining up at the gate, the third-show audience could be seen in a widening line, six abreast, appearing to go out to infinity. The show was going to be a big success, but we had to fix our act.

It was clear that the supposedly foolproof baseball sketch had not connected with the audience. It had offended some portion of the crowd and caused them to turn off for the rest of the show. I approached Mahatta and said, "Mahatta-san! You are the expert; you must know your people. Please tell me why do *you* think the audience went away so fast?"

He stopped walking, looked around to see who else might overhear, then said, "You know American baseball, you do not know Japanese baseball. To you baseball is a pastime, in Japan baseball is more important." He stormed off.

I saw a couple of American servicemen standing in line to get into the second show. I felt like a goof, but I approached them. "Hi there. As you can see I'm a clown with the circus, could I ask you guys for some help?" *They* had attended a Japanese baseball game, something I had foolishly neglected to do, and kindly explained the differences between American and Japanese pregame rituals and players' responses to hits, runs, and errors.

I called an emergency rehearsal. With less than an hour before the next show, we added some ritual moves to our interpretation of baseball and, just to be safe, inserted a bit of a popular native folk dance we had learned the first night we arrived. The Japanese found it funny, though I was not sure why. No matter, now we were a hit!

Business was soon booming for the All-American Circus. After our rough opening, we got into a groove, doing three shows a day for about forty-five thousand delighted ticket buyers and getting outstandingly good publicity. The Mainichi newspaper was one of our sponsors—E. K. Fernandez saw to that. The Daiei Motion Picture Company—the producers of *Rashomon*—decided to shoot a Japanese version of *Romeo and Juliet*, set in modern Japan, using the All-American Circus as one of the locations.

Doc had been featured in a lot of the advertising for the show. His good-natured Tramp character—"I'm penniless but oh so happy, not a care in the world, I'm free because I'm broke"—seemed to resonate with the audience and became an easy symbol for the word *circus*. Doc and I were beginning to enjoy a growing fan club of mostly female admirers when the movie opened. Six weeks after the last day of principal photography, our fan club grew to several thousand, mostly young, and mostly female.

Doc's attitude toward the Japanese had gone from war crazy to saying, "These really are nice folks, once you get to know them." Michiko Ute should get the credit for turning Doc's head and heart around. She was liaison between the U.S. Army Intelligence and the Daiei brass and spent most days at the circus. After a while. she was spending her nights there as well.

If there had been no Pearl Harbor, if there had been no war, the 1942 Olympic Games would have been held in the elegant stadium in Nishinomiya, Japan, where the All-American Circus was presented nearly a decade later. The influence of the other Axis powers was very much visible and intentional, a mix of classic marble and Mussolini modern. The location, centered between Osaka, Kobe, and Kyoto, guaranteed even larger audiences than Tokyo. The producers, the U.S government, and E. K. were all looking forward to the move to the south of Japan and to continued success. But then I made a well-meaning but foolish mistake that nearly destroyed the circus.

The Office of Strategic Services (OSS) brass did not bother to let all of the performers in on the fact that the Japanese royal household had reserved special seats for the Tokyo matinee, only a few weeks before the official lifting of the U.S. occupation. All was not tranquil. There had been May Day riots and a few burning cars, but no one expected things to worsen once the occupation was officially over and American soldiers started going home.

We were presenting the circus in a structure that had been built for sumo wrestling and was designed to accommodate the masses. These huge audiences were a challenge to play to; it was hard to get close when the layout put so many people high up in the stands. Most of the audience was kimono clad and sat on their knees for more than two hours. A few people in Western dress would be seated in actual chairs along the front side of the track.

The bandleader, Ramón, blew the trumpet announcing the half hour, so Punch and I started working the front rail. The house was about two-thirds full as we worked our way along the special red seats. I was honking my greetings, shaking a few hands, getting a few laughs, and having a good time. Just in front of the center ring I stopped, tipped my hat, made a lean-in bow, reached out, and shook the hand of a polite, short, very well-dressed young man about my age. I honked my horns in time to the up and down of our handshake and ended as usual with the bell. He was smiling a shy smile and gave a little giggle. The young woman next to him covered her mouth in that charming way Japanese women stifle open laughter. Flashbulbs popped, and the audience that had been laughing went absolutely silent for a moment.

Then about ten thousand people gave an alarmed gasp and began an embarrassed murmuring. Two very tall men who must have been from Hokkaido stepped forward, glaring at me. I continued to move along the rail. The young man laughed a little louder, the tall guys sat back down, and the crowd let out a sigh. That sigh so surprised everyone that they began laughing at their own surprise. Still not knowing what had happened, I worked my way around to the performers' entrance, the show began, and I headed for the dressing room.

"What was that?" Doc asked. "The crowd just went dead; I could hear them just freeze up from here."

Before I could answer, Walter Mahatta and a security guy stormed in, spewing orders in Japanese, swearing every profanity that he knew in English and inventing new words to fit the occasion.

"You! You touched the Crown Prince! No one! No one touches any member of the royal family!" He rattled off something in Japanese, trying to justify himself with the head of security. "Thousands of years—no one is allowed to touch the royal family!"

E. K. arrived and said, "No one is supposed to go anywhere near, much less touch, any member of the royal household. You just touched Akihito, the Crown Prince, the son of Emperor Hirohito."

"The son of the Son of the Sun God!" Mahatta piped in.

Men in suits were all over the backyard. Uniformed Japanese cops and U.S. Army brass were all trying to get control of the situation without knowing *which* situation. I looked at Doc, he nodded, and silently spoke *snafu*: "situation normal, all fouled up."

Mahatta came up to me real close, looked around, and said very quietly, "I think I'll be able to get you out of the country. Not sure yet, but you need to know that I'll try to do everything I can to keep you safe. Trust me."

E. K. walked in with a grim look on his almost always cheerful face. "Son, you can't go back to the Ga Joa Inn tonight. The anti-Royalists and the Communists, everybody is just going nuts. The Jap secret-service guys are trying to arrest each other, so the army liaison people are sending some of their security."

"Thank God we still have control," said some army major. "If the occupation was lifted, who knows what would have happened? If this had happened in prewar Japan, all twelve of those secret-service guys protecting the prince would have been ordered to commit hara-kiri. It's only because we still have some control and can take some of the blame and because of the new constitution that these guys will be allowed to live. Except some of them might do themselves in just out of pride and force of habit."

"You!" Mahatta addressed me. "You are out of the show. Take off your makeup."

Two army officers took me to their office.

"You can bunk down on the major's couch," one of them said. "There are MPs here all the time, so relax until we decide what to do with you."

The next morning, Mahatta came in and told me that because Freddy and his flying troupe had *accidentally* walked on the red carpet that they had been fired and were already at Pan Am waiting for their flight home. E. K. brought the morning newspapers. The picture showing Akihito shaking my hand was great, but the editorials were all nasty:

American Arrogance

U. S. Violates . . .

Not Amused by Yank Joke

This was an international crisis. Nationalists and anti-Royalists both used the situation to air their anti-American rants. I had "offended Japan," and now I was in big trouble. Everyone with an ax to grind found the situation a handy peg on which to hang their anti-American rants. I was feeling pretty bad, thinking about packing up. Then I felt worse when I realized that if I got deported, Doc would lose his job too, because we were in on a single-family passport. So much for trying to save a few bucks.

For three days I thought of myself as an unpatriotic American who had disgraced the Riggs family name, wrecked the tour, and bankrupted the All-American Circus. Then the

Mainichi newspaper printed an editorial that quoted a bulletin from the Royal Palace that defused the situation:

"The photo does not insult the royal family. To the contrary, the photo reflects the New Japan. A Japan that reaches out to the West, a Japan that reaches out the hand of friendship to the World." Perhaps our handshake signaled a change.

"We are going to keep all of this very quiet," Mahatta said. "You are very lucky, but don't get too cocky. I still have your Pan Am ticket in my pocket."

FLIFFUS IT IS!

The happiest time I could remember; I was smitten.

When the E. K. Fernandez All-American Circus tour ended in Manila, I boarded the Scandinavian motor ship *Fernland* and for twenty-eight days, nothing was required of me. Oddly, that stimulated a great deal of creative energy and discussion about theater, art, and music, especially jazz. The *Fernland* was a co-pra cargo vessel and allowed a complement of no more than twelve passengers because there was no doctor on board. The passenger roster listed eight other Fernandez Circus performers, including my dad and Paul Bornjorno and Marylyn Rice, as well as our Japanese PR man, and an American musician named Bernie Sailor.

Bernie was returning to San Francisco, rejoining his jazz life, which included selling arrangements to the Ellington big band. "I'm taking the slow boat back so that I can work on some new arrangements," he said. When we first met at the ship's breakfast cold table (lots of cheese, fish, and pickled things offered several times a day by two very attractive Swedish stewardesses), I heard that he had attended our circus and knew many of the performers. Marylyn Rice knew Bernie from some earlier shared tour, and they seemed like they would be good people to be friends with. I could see that they would be easy friends. The *Fernland*'s Captain Neilson seated Bernie, Marylyn, and me at his table the first night (an honor I assumed he would rotate with other passengers throughout the voyage). This arrangement generated a most productive month of conversation, debate, and civilized discussion centered on "rational ways to solve all the world's problems," and it forged some lasting friendships that led to Fliffus.

Normally, I kept pretty close counsel, not burdening others with anything personal. I caught myself ruminating about all the choices I had to make. I had too many "shouldas": I should have stayed in school. I should get back to the Riggs & Riggs career. I should not be taking these bookings because that slows down college and keeps me from getting where I want to be.

Marylyn interrupted my wailing. "Just where is that?" she asked. This was actually a serious question, put directly to me. "Where is that 'place' you want to be?"

Her candor put me off balance. "I don't know."

Bernie leaned over and said, "That is not a good answer!"

I explained the problem of my being caught between my mother's constant reminder to "stay in school and be prepared for life" and my father's belief that "show business is life!" I told them that it seemed natural that I would follow my father into the family business.

These two new friends were good listeners and could have just said, "There, there" or something neutral and avoided getting involved in the problems of who? After all, I had just met Bernie.

Bernie took a while and then said, "Yes, but . . ." He moved to sit next to Marylyn. They were both looking me in the eye. Bernie said, "You *do* have free will."

Marylyn said, "After all, you aren't *chained* to the Riggs family business."

Thus began the most honest talks that I had ever had. These were show people, but they were grown-up show people, confident of their talent, and not needing the froth of small talk.

Marylyn like to talk about "the good, the true, and the beautiful." She was always questioning. She said she loved debating. "Not arguing, just formal discussion and debate. I like to exercise my mind," she said.

"What is truth?" I asked.

"Truth is fragile, it comes apart easily and fragmentary pieces of truth fall off exposing a greater—no, a lesser truth? Now I'm not sure. We must explore. Pieces of truth that cling and pieces that fall off. Sometimes you have to pick up all the little pieces that were lost."

"How can we have more than one truth?" asked Bernie.

"We all see the same thing at the same time, but the truth we each see is remembered as different truths. Is that right?"

This was all new to me. They always put an idea forward as a question. Avoid the absolutes. This was exciting, productive talk.

"And memory of truth is not infallible?" I asked.

"It's human nature," said Bernie. "I have a theory. I think that every time you pull something out of past memory, you revise it a little. So an oft-repeated story is constantly revised. Does that make it richer truth?"

I was still a sophomore and out of my depth, but happy to be included.

Marylyn picked up on Bernie's theme. "We must think our revisions make for a richer story. If that's true, is it a truer truth?"

"I'm not sure that it makes for a better truth. I'm always skeptical when I hear someone claim to know some absolute truth and know all of the facts. Always swearing up and down that they are only speaking the truth."

She looked at Bernie and smiled. Then she looked me straight in the eye and said, "Now if we're talking about romantic love, I take back everything I just said."

Marylyn was a one-of-a-kind woman. I had never met anyone even remotely like her. She was not a woman willing to play dumb for the benefit of male egos. She never played that towner girl trick of asking a feigned serious question about something when anyone could see that she already knew the answer.

Both Bernie and Marylyn seemed so curious and open to new ideas that I chattered away, trotting out more and more fanciful "what if" ideas, half expecting Bernie to interrupt with "Enough of your crazy ideas." But he did not interrupt! He smiled and continued to listen quietly for a while before he said, "I like to understand what you are saying before I take the floor. If I have nothing new to add, why stir the confusion? Please continue."

That was an unexpected and new experience for me. I grew up with show people, a group that was inclined to speak in the contradictory shorthand style that kept conversations short and sometimes intentionally free of meaning.

With Bernie, I found that *not* being interrupted was a bit unnerving. I watched my pauses expectantly, staying only half committed to my point until it dawned on me: This is a real friend. I don't need to be on guard because he's not on guard. We are not trying to one-up each other with man-to-man challenge games. We can actually have a polite, friendly conversation, respecting each other, even when we disagree about the subject.

They provided corrections to flawed logic and gently pushed me to examine my positions, always in a positive, open, and friendly way. And they listened to me. Most people can't listen because they are so busy interrupting. Bernie Sailor taught me a new way to understand the public and how to disarm an audience by the simple act of listening to them. Learning to listen, really listen, later became the key to all successful audience participation work.

As I got more confident about holding my own with these older, obviously passionate, smart people, I began sprouting some less-thought-through ideas. "Maybe it would be possible to blend classical ballet with circus aerial: Tchaikovsky's ballet score and a love story high in the air. A circus act with a plot."

Bernie was very kind: he would listen to what I had to say, then softly echo the words back to me, sometimes with a slightly quizzical look. Marylyn was welcoming and friendly but direct: "Don't you think Tchaikovsky would be difficult for the circus band since they have so few violins?"

At first I felt obliged to not bore her or reveal my lack of maturity, but after a few hours the sense of age difference had faded, and I realized I was smitten with this (only slightly) older woman.

We began discussing good jazz, bad opera, and my idea of using the new Freudian concept of "free association" to create stage dialogue. I brought up The Humanettes and how my folks often fielded audience suggestions and ran with them to buy time. We talked about how it might be possible to riff ideas off the top of our heads, to build a dialogue the way jazz players riff and repeat musical phrases.

Marylyn said, "You mean ad-lib the whole bit? Without a script or a prompter? Why would you do that?"

Bernie said, "Why not?" He paused for a moment and then said, "Why the hell not?"

The subject had never gotten very far in school discussions before it became an easy tool for a put-down. I thought Marylyn and Bernie would think it through and not rush to quick judgment or the oh-so-easy joke.

"Free association makes me think of hypnosis and psychotherapy and too much unresolved stuff," Marylyn said.

Bernie smiled, with eyes wide. "I think of crazy laughter, Dalí, and Ingrid Bergman."

"You think it has too much baggage?" I asked.

"Maybe you should find some safe, neutral way to describe 'Your Thing.'" He was dismissive as he paused for a long beat. "Or just drop the subject."

That stung. I said my goodnights and retired. I spent the long night ranting to myself, trying to understand what caused the chill from my friends and trying to think of meaningless words to replace what Bernie called "Your Thing." Searching for a neutral word or phrase, I finally decided the word would be "Fliffus."

Usually known only to aerialists, the term "Fliffus" describes a difficult, complicated, but beautiful flying act feat. Shamefully, I had never successfully completed the flying Fliffus. Maybe that's why it came to mind when I was looking for a word to describe a new kind of theater that I began to envision. I needed a neutral phrase because every time I used the term "free association," which carried the connotation of Freud and psychoanalysis, people went nuts. I suppose they thought I wanted to expose their secret thoughts. And the term "improvisation," the musicians insisted, belonged rightly to jazz. So I came up with my own word for it and Fliffus it was.

In this way, serendipity led to the eventual development of the first incarnation of what later became my brand of improvisational theater.

"Why not?" I thought. "Why not" might just be pretty good words to live by.

I was so impressed by these people. Marylyn: so warm and friendly, always lighting up the room with her smile. Bernie: smart, open-minded, and fearless when it came to trying new things.

From my earliest memories as a child on the road, traveling from city to city, my family made a pastime of playing what my grandmother called Roundelay, a verbal word game. To help the driver stay awake on long hauls, we would each take our turn, adding personal feelings to the ongoing fantasy story. "Now, remember, listen, think, and speak clearly. All these little tales joined together can become a single grand fantasy, created by many authors," said my grandmother. "Not unlike the Scriptures."

And not unlike improvisational theater.

Reciting aloud, we each added our part, inspired by what we knew of the story so far. And when we ran out of breath or ideas, we took a pause, by inserting "who . . ." The next person would use "who" as the first word to continue the tale. This sometimes went on for hours as we traveled the three or four hundred miles to get to the next engagement.

When Bernie first heard me talking about Roundelay, he came alive with excitement and took on Grandmother Riggs' word game with almost patriotic zeal. We talked late into the night when the only other sound was the steady hum of the *Fernland*'s engines and the hourly time bells. Bernie talked about Greek theater and South American music. Marylyn brought up acting and acting teachers, Lee Strasberg, and The Method. "It's the new thing in New York."

Speaking to what we each thought qualified as "new and original," we laughed and argued into the predawn. Often not about things new, just things new to me.

What a revelation. That one month on the *Fernland* with Marylyn and Bernie was the happiest block of time I could remember. Doc saw it differently: "The Riggs Brothers lost a month of work when you decided to turn in our Pan Am tickets." He kept forgetting that our rigging had to go surface, by water, and the month would be lost either way.

When we docked in San Francisco, I said good-bye to my new friends and promised to keep in touch.

★ 10 ★

WORD JAZZ

"It just might become something wonderful."

When we returned to the United States after our 1952 Asian tour, we were at the top of our game, feeling flush and expecting some big-time offers, but something had changed. The American circus was in decline. Television had put vaudeville in a coma, and fairs were down, but the nightclub business was picking up, hiring variety acts for supper-club revue productions.

Doc had a short booking on the Gil Gray Circus, but I was at liberty, so I went back to college in Mankato, Minnesota, for a while, assuming that show business would soon recover.

Chuck McKinsey, my roommate in the dorm, endlessly quizzed me about why the trip had so transformed my thinking and fired my sudden enthusiasm for *modern* jazz.

"When you left, you loved Dixieland jazz. What happened to you?"

I probably repeated every word of every conversation I'd had with Marylyn and Bernie. Chuck proved that he too was a good listener, but he was always diligent in reminding me that there was a reason we were attending classes.

My college friends often challenged my thinking about where I was putting my creative energy because they didn't know or care about show business. In my mind, I was caught between the exciting world of show business and immediate job offers and years of college with just the possibility of a teaching career. I had made this callow calculation: if I work really hard, I should be able to get my college education without interrupting the Riggs family performance schedule. I had been so busy performing that I had not taken the time to think things through.

In March, I heard that Marylyn and Bernie had landed a job in Minneapolis, playing and singing modern jazz in the lounge at the Radisson Hotel. So I started doing a weekly commute up to the Twin Cities to hear my friends perform. The second week they graciously invited me to sit in during their set.

They performed a forty-minute musical set, singing sly little calypso songs and playing modern jazz. I was impressed by Bernie's loose, four-line nonsense phrase pieces with percussion backing and Marylyn's absolutely clear singing voice. They suggested that "as a change of pace," I should do my act billed as "Five minutes of juggling and comedy patter," memorized one-line gags punctuated by drum and cymbal crashes. To my surprise, I got a good reception from the nicely dressed dinner crowd. The audience seemed pleased to be there even when we tried ideas that didn't work (as when I tried to recite poetry to Bernie's jazz in time with my juggling moves).

Mostly I enjoyed being reunited with my friends from the *Fernland.* Marylyn and Bernie were supportive and generous. They treated me like I was some kind of crazy guest star who dropped by bringing fun and surprises—a guest who needed an audience, some stage time, and some protective shelter. "You can do whatever you are big enough to do," Marylyn said. "Just don't get us arrested."

Whenever I came up with a new gag, Bernie said, "Why not?" That was such a gift of creative freedom. That openness and the challenge to try out ideas soon began to produce some actual comedy. I was being kept awake by a constant flow of "what if" queries. Each new audience taught me something fresh.

Then one night in the third week, when the audience was especially warm and receptive, Bernie surprised me when he said, "It's 'showtime,' D. R.! Time for *us* to do a bit *together.* This is a good audience to test that top-of-the-head, ad-lib bit of yours."

Marylyn was protective and concerned. "You guys can't just walk on stage naked without script or props!" she said.

"Why not? I play jazz without sides. The notes come to me as I play," Bernie said.

That first night, with Marylyn on piano, Bernie and I tried making up a story, one word at a time, batting words back and forth like ping-pong. It was not much of a start. To the confused audience it came off a little awkward and unfriendly.

We were trying way too hard to look cool and clever and to top each other's lines.

Later Marylyn spoke kindly. "You guys were interesting . . . but this was not what one could call entertainment."

I thought: "Interesting. Why not just say 'You flopped!'"

"You boys just need to take the time to hear each other and think before you speak. And you should try being nice to each other!"

Two weeks later, this short ad-lib interval between musical sets was judged to be less of an irritating interruption for the audience. Some said they "enjoyed the change of pace."

Marylyn, who was having fun making the intro and building up the audience, said, "Let's call it Word Play or Word Dance. It needs a cute, catchy name if it's going to catch on."

We were still making halting mistakes, but as in jazz, we repeated the mistakes, laughing and having fun, and seeing this somehow infected the crowd. "Are they laughing at us or with us?" asked Bernie.

"It does not matter one whit, as long as they're laughing," said Marylyn.

The club used the title "Ad Lib Ad Absurdum" for a month. I spent the weekend commutes doing these short stints in front of the club audience, testing new bits and training my voice. After years of pantomime performing, I was finally using my voice onstage again.

I still hadn't figured out how to make the ad-lib duet sustain for more than a few minutes at a time. Marylyn's intro took more stage time than the bit itself, and even with the light jazz support, it still felt short.

Then Marylyn suggested we try working less cool and detached by turning and looking directly face-to-face. "Be friendly. Be polite. Listen harder. Smile more. If you have fun, the audience has fun."

We talked after every show, practiced our delivery, but avoided talking about the future. Bernie didn't need me. And he certainly didn't need my crazy "talk" piece. He had cheerfully indulged my "thing" out of friendship, but I knew that he would drop it if we had one too many bad shows.

Once we could read and anticipate each other, the flow improved, and the stories got longer and began to actually make sense. Marylyn was beaming. "It's almost like religion," she said. Bernie believed in jazz. I believed in free association. Marylyn believed in art, beauty, and good manners. We talked long and hard and agreed to continue.

I said we should bill it "Word Jazz."

On Saturday nights, right after the break when the lounge crowd was predictably relaxed and willing to participate, Marylyn set up the audience by asking for single-word suggestions, which she listed on a blackboard. The club patrons were only mildly interested until the lights went down, and she made the simple understated announcement: "And now . . . Ladies and Gentlemen . . . Word Jazz."

Standing back-to-back in a tight spotlight, Bernie and I took turns reciting what was advertised as "a made-up-on-the-spot story," starting with that single word suggested by someone in the audience. The trick was always to honor the given word and try to inflect some meaning into the connections.

One night it went like this: the audience-supplied word was *whiskey*, so *prohibition* logically came to mind as the second word. Then *Al Capone*. Then back and forth for about fifty words as we each took our turn responding to the previous word. Often and ideally, the lead word would circle back, so that *depression, divorce,* would carry the story back to the cause of it all, which was *whiskey*. A sad story that starts with whiskey and ends in divorce.

When we spoke the last two words, we'd turn and face each other, shake hands, and take our bow. The story did not always have a point, but the audience applauded while we struggled, nearly out of breath, to make meaning out of random words. Soon we found that we could dazzle the audience with speed and vocal dexterity, but the story still needed to make some kind of sense. That was the hard part.

When we tried to graduate from single-word exchanges to full sentences, we embarrassed ourselves in front of a friendly crowd. Suddenly tongue-tied, we verbally walked all over each other before Marylyn killed the lights. The audience laughed *at* us that night.

Being laughed off the stage is not at all pleasant. If this were to happen again, I knew that Bernie would walk away from my act with no regrets. Bernie was fearless but not foolish. We had gotten overconfident and underestimated the heft of the task. I needed to go back to the basics.

I thought: Responding to each single word is easy.

"His word" cued "my word." "My word" cued "his word."

A single word (usually), a small amount of meaning.

But sentences are loaded with meaning.

"His sentence" cued "my sentence." That's harder.

Marylyn was right; this was not as simple as I thought.

There is still a lot . . . of work to do.

We were getting better every week, but by spring I was trying to finish classes and book circus dates for The Riggs Brothers. Marylyn and Bernie moved to Chicago to take other jobs. They each promised to keep in touch, and I promised to call them if I ever had paying work.

My friends from the *Fernland* had never stopped asking me, "What do you really want to do? Really?" All through that winter as I commuted up to the Cities to be with Marylyn and Bernie, I was asking myself that question.

When I returned to Mankato, I enrolled in an education department class titled "Stage Direction for Educational Theater," aimed primarily at future high-school teachers. Students in my theater direction class were always talking theory and all manner of utopian dreams: plays they wanted to see, plays that would be fun to do, plays that they absolutely must direct. The list contained plays from every historical period and style from the past two thousand years, a vast canon of work that was overwhelming to me. I realized how little I knew about the great playwrights of the past and the beauty of theatrical literature. I was so busy *doing* shows, I missed *seeing* shows. I had missed how essential the playwright was to the play.

My professor said, "First, the play has to be written, then, at a later time, after countless hours of work, it can be performed for an audience. It's a process of many steps." My head was still stuck, ruminating about the possibility of writing the play *while* performing it. So, in the hope of getting extra credit, I decided to test my Fliffus notion.

So I posted a request for volunteer subjects on the theater department announcement board. I cobbled together an exercise that I hoped would make Fliffus legitimate. I thought I might get credit, maybe even acceptance. Here is what I told them:

Exploring Fliffus: A Creative Tool

This script was chosen because it's stilted and stiff. No one talks this way anymore, as if anyone ever did. Let's see if it's possible to make it more conversational, like real people talk, more relaxed, more honest.

You each have been given a copy of the script.

Now, here's what I want you to do for me: Ignore the title.

Do a quick cursory read through of the script. Read it again, thinking about your character. Really think about your character.

Now I want you to do the scene without the script.

You now know your characters; you know where the story is going, so I want you to do the play without script but with your imagination engaged. Don't try to remember the old lines, just create new lines.

Allow yourself to move about. It's ok to be open, spontaneous, and even a little wild. Don't worry about going up on lines; you don't have to memorize these lines because they are soon going to be replaced by your lines. As you walk through the scene, do what your character does, but let the words come off the top of your head. Keep an open mind.

Use the first word that comes into your mind, and don't worry about the words being the right words. These are your words so they are the right words. I'm looking for real, honest expression, based on how you and your character feel right now. This is a group enterprise; let yourself be part of the group.

Allow your smartest self to stay in control. Avoid cheap shot conflicts. Don't stop and judge what comes out. Keep going. Keep listening. Hear what's said with an open mind. Everyone needs to know that their speech is respected. Remember, everyone has free speech even when you disagree with what they say. Once you hear it all, you may change your view.

Try to think Positively Neutral.

Try to suspend judgment about yourself and others. Be nice. Have fun.

Let the story go where it wants to go. Listen to each other, and build on what you hear. We may end up with a totally different scene, and the scene may change your character. That's good. We have to trust each other and not try to upstage each other. Help each other.

We are all writing this script together. It does not have to tell the old story; it should tell a new story that is the combined expression from each of you and all of us. Allow yourself the freedom to create something new even if it's just here today, gone tomorrow. This is new to me, too. It's just an idea being developed. We are trying something that I think can work.

Your hardest task is to not judge what you're doing.

We don't know what this will look like when it's finished, but let's have some fun and see where it goes. It might just become something wonderful.

I received a curt note from my professor. "Observing your project, I couldn't help thinking that the time and energy of these students could have been more wisely invested in the study of a more serious subject." My interest in improvisation was seen as an avoidance of the real task of a theater student. In addition, I hadn't yet realized that I needed to create an environment where this approach could work. It wasn't well developed at this stage. There's nothing so bad as a great notion that didn't work.

The original script called for four women and three men and was selected at random from the school's play library. Some of the student volunteers hated the idea at first but warmed to it by the third try after they'd gotten to know each other and that extra credit might also be shared.

Some of my fellow students probably thought that I was a nut case. Fortunately, there were two Korean War vets there on the GI Bill, who were older than the rest and willing to take direction. They calmed the class. I was still standing out as the oddball to these students, all of whom wanted a teaching degree or a "Mrs. Degree." Coeds were friendly until they learned that I would leave when I got another show-biz opportunity.

★ 11 ★

NEVER LET THEM
KNOW YOU CAN
DRIVE A SEMI

I get another show-business "opportunity."

That following spring, I was hired to be the center-ring star of a small but prestigious circus for a tour along the Alcan Highway in Canada. This was an opportunity to reach and entertain a new audience for circus and earn a large salary.

Circus tours usually avoid moving heavy trucks and heavy elephants into the mountains. The show's truck drivers were constantly complaining about the long mileage jumps and hazards of overheating the brakes and the terror of an uncontrolled runaway rig that you can't stop.

I didn't have to worry about all that. As a privileged performing artist, I had the free time and was enjoying the beauty of the mountains from my own English sports car.

One hot afternoon I had just passed a 9,200-foot elevation sign when I came upon the show's "Number 7" truck, stalled with a blown motor. There was a huge hole in the hood, and the thrown pistons, which came to rest on the road about fifty feet away, had shattered the windshield. The black smoke, colored by the patrol car's flashing lights, and the endless pacing back and forth by the big cats in the trailer lent a fearful seriousness to the scene.

Angry roars from the caged animals prompted the newly arrived Mountie to unsnap the flap covering his revolver.

The stainless-steel cages housed ten cats in all: three Bengal tigers, a puma, a leopard, a black-maned Nubian lion, and the four females of his pride. These were display animals, too old to work in a circus performance but still providing a menagerie display.

The truck driver—a guy I knew as Charlie—was hanging plywood curtains over the bars and chattering to himself out loud. "I told them that this would need a new motor if we were going to do these mountains. I told them. Now that cop is freaking out about the cats. I got to keep them quiet so that jerk doesn't go nuts and shoot them in their cage." Charlie tended to get nervous around authority.

The curtains seemed to calm the cats, so Charlie cooled down as well. The Mountie, however, was still on high alert, having picked up the agitated pacing of the cats.

The owner of the show and the show's lawyer were already there, talking to the captain of the Royal Canadian Mounted Police and making plans to have the rig towed to the nearest town that had a Mack truck garage. There would be no performances and a delay of several days until a new motor could be located and installed. This was going to be a very expensive repair job and had to be paid with cash because no one would likely accept a check from itinerate show people. And there was another problem: the show was always short on big-rig truck drivers and Charlie—while being one of the very best— was not someone to leave behind in a town with a liquor store and in charge of so much money.

The owner walked close to me and said: "I've decided to leave Charlie here with the truck and leave you here with the money to pay for the new motor. I just don't trust Charlie to stay sober. So *you* are in charge. The show needs you. Get the motor in and try to catch up with the show by the time we play Saskatoon."

A large paper sack full of cash was thrust into my hand, then the owner said a polite good-bye to me and made a challenge to Charlie to stay sober. With that, he and the lawyer drove on up the mountain before I thought of saying no.

Charlie got a room in the hotel near the Mack garage replacing the motor. Twelve miles higher up the mountain, I found a place to tow the trailer portion of the rig and waited with the very smelly and hungry residents of the menagerie.

There were about nine hundred pounds of frozen horse-meat in the trailer freezer and no lack of enthusiasm at feeding time. As a trapeze flyer, I had no experience with animal acts, and this was really not my job, but Charlie was down in the valley and the roaring had to be kept under control to keep the Mounties away.

Each day I'd check on the motor and look in on Charlie, who was usually asleep or out of his room. I'd have a Chinese meal in one of three Chinese cafés in the small town and check the weather predicted for Saskatoon. On the fourth day, the truck was ready.

Cash from the paper sack paid for the new motor, and we were good to go. I'd just go get Charlie, hook up the trailer, and we would be ready to roll south to Saskatoon.

Going up the stairs of the Hoy Toy Hotel I could hear a lot of strident chatter in three-part disharmony. A twentyish Chinese woman, an older Chinese man, and a very young girl were all shouting at once. Charlie was drunk and mumbling something about not knowing how the girl got into his room. A man with a baseball bat shouted, "You go now! You Go! NOW you go!"

I paid the hotel bill, apologized to the management, and tried to get Charlie over to the garage to pick up the truck. As he staggered past the Mountie station, the sergeant called out, "Which one of you fellows is the driver for that circus truck?"

Charlie couldn't answer. I said, in my very best legal voice, "He's the driver, but of course he won't be driving tonight. We only have to rejoin the show in Saskatoon in a few days. We plan to cross over the pass, pick up 37, go down past Prince George, and take 16 all the way to Saskatoon."

The sergeant looked at the map, laughed a little laugh, and, gesturing in my direction, said something to the others, who promptly broke up as if they had seen me take a pratfall.

"I think you may have to revise your plan, son."

The laughter ended. The Mountie was now quite serious.

"You most likely will have to delay your trip, or try to reroute yourself back through the States. You won't get to Highway 37 because the ferry crossing closes at midnight tonight. Looks like you boys might be with us for quite a while," the sergeant said in a kind voice. Then he turned back, all business: "Don't even consider letting that drunk drive—today, tonight, or even next week." He was obviously angry with Charlie, and I later learned there had been several police calls during his short stay at the Hoy Toy Hotel. Charlie had easily worn out our welcome.

It was about 1,200 miles to Saskatoon, and if we had to go back down into the States and then back up into Saskatchewan, our trip would more than double. By the time we caught up, the show would have moved on to somewhere else. We absolutely had to make that ferry before midnight.

I chatted with the mechanic, asking about the mountain, and he quickly got ahead of me: "You ain't gonna try and drive this yourself, son? I mean, you do have a driver, don't you?'"

I assured him that Charlie had over a million miles on the road. "He is a fully professional driver," I said. *When he is sober,* I thought to myself.

It was now Saturday afternoon; Charlie was sleeping it off in the sleeping compartment behind the cab. The rig was gassed and ready. I figured it was time for Charlie to start doing his job. A half-drunk experienced driver who knows how to drive the truck trumps a totally inept terrified driver any day, right?

When I opened the sleeper compartment hatch, an acid mist of gin and vomit blew into my face.

"Hey!" yelled Charlie. "Are you ready for a little drink?' He was happily singing a drinking song.

Charlie was now the drunkest I had ever seen him.

"Just relax, Charlie, I'll be back with some coffee in a little while."

I closed the hatch and locked it.

I considered my situation. Charlie was ten years older and about eighty pounds heavier than me with a lot of facial scars. Taking Charlie's bottle away from him did not seem like an option. I got behind the wheel and stared at the dashboard. My anger at Charlie was tame next to the anger at myself for leaving college again for show business.

I started the engine and drove slow circles around the parking lot, trying to talk myself into believing that I could drive, but never getting out of second gear.

I had been told that missing a shift could be the beginning of a very fast freewheeling ride off the edge of this dangerously steep mountain.

I put small Band-Aid markers on the tachometer, marking shift points for each of the gears. I was terrified that blowing a shift or overusing the brakes would end our lives.

I *was* terrified, but I had to drive.

The Canadian Rockies are inspiring during the day, but at night the beauty gets lost in the uncertainty of not knowing where you are.

It started to rain, and the road was getting slippery. On one curve I could see the trailer section growing larger in my side mirror as the heavier end tried to catch up and pass the tractor end. I started to brake, but luckily I accidently hit the gas, which, like magic, straightened the whole unit, and I made the curve.

That could have been fatal, I thought. This trip could be my last. This had been a whole series of my lasts. If I make a last mistake, I could be responsible for the deaths of two humans and a lot of exotic endangered wildlife.

After five hours of steady white-knuckle travel, I saw the sign for Watson's Lake Ferry Crossing.

Ta-da! I made it!

It was almost eleven o'clock. Such a great feeling. I felt like taking a bow.

But as I made it down toward the lake, the bigger trucks were passing me, their drivers looking angry as they rushed to get a place in the line. All the trucks that passed me were now parked in a single file on a fifteen-foot-wide roadbed that had been bulldozed through the very dense forest sloping down to the L-shaped ferry landing. A Royal Canadian Mounted Police officer, in full uniform and with a flashlight and clipboard, was telling each new arrival what was required. He pointed across the river and yelled:

"The only way to get off the ferry over there is to drive straight off. That means you have to back your semi up onto the ferry now." There was a collective groan as he pointed toward the boat. "I know it's real narrow, but you guys are all first-class drivers or you wouldn't be here, right?"

Not quite right.

I started to argue with myself. What to do? I'm in deep trouble. No way can I back this truck onto that boat. I haven't ever been able to back it up *at all*. I'll go over the side, sink in the lake, and never be seen again. The show will fold, and if I am ever seen again, it will be in some Canadian jail for impersonating a truck driver.

Then I had a change of trouble.

The trucks were starting to move again, and I would soon be first in line.

Some drivers were quarrelsome, yelling to get the line moving, eager to beat the midnight deadline. The truck behind my Mack was a huge Peterbilt loaded with giant logs. Its driver, also huge, was dressed in black studded leather and a cap with the name "Skagg" embroidered on the visor. He was telling his buddy, "Mack's not a real truck." He acted offended. "That sissy rig shouldn't even be in the company of serious work trucks."

He was looking directly at me. He knew that I could hear him.

So it looked like he wanted to hold court and have a little fun on my tab. He gestured toward me, nodded to the other drivers, said something under his breath, and they all laughed.

Damn! After such a fun trip, now I get to meet the rough trade. I'm up to my nose in trouble. What to do?

My only thought: "Don't sing."

I took a deep breath and walked back past my trailer toward the men and said, "Hi there."

Skagg just stared. I walked closer and said, "How long have you been driving truck?"

"Whaat?" His face flushed up.

The other drivers moved in closer, mumbling confusion and speculation, clearly hoping to see some action.

Now I really was in trouble.

I found my deepest and loudest voice. "HOW LONG HAVE YOU BEEN DRIVING TRUCK?"

"Sixteen years, not that it's any of your damned business!"

"Well, sir," I said in a very quiet voice, "I have been driving this truck for only five hours, and that is the total of my truck-driving experience. I really don't know how to drive it, and I absolutely know that I will not be able to back it down that narrow gangway. I will not be able to get on that ferry and that ferry is going to go soon."

What'd he say? What's going on? Everybody was edging for a fight or laughing at me.

I made a loud announcement: "I do not know how to back up this truck!"

I moved up to Skagg.

"So I think you should do us both a big favor and back my truck onto the ferry. I'm next, and if I don't get on . . . none of you get on."

I took three steps back, and for some unknown reason, slapped the side curtain for emphasis.

This woke the sleeping cats.

Raja did a spitting hiss and lunged against the bars, shaking the cage. That caused the leopards to answer the growls. I slapped other cage covers until King, the big male lion, woke up his pride and decided to drown out the other cats. Soon all four breeds of jungle cats were drowning out the jeering laughter. Things had changed.

Wild jungle cats were blocking their semis.

Skagg didn't say a word. He pushed past me, climbed aboard my Mack, fired up the engine, gave a blast on the air horns, and backed the truck onto the ferry.

———•———

Four hundred uneventful miles later, Charlie was once again sober. We stopped at a truck stop, and he got cleaned up, bought a new shirt, and pointedly stayed away from the beer cooler. I turned over the keys *only* after we exchanged promises: I promised not to tell the boss about his drinking and the Hoy Toy Hotel. He promised not to tell the owner that I knew anything about driving a semi.

We arrived in Saskatoon a day late and only a few dollars short. I wondered if I should go back to college, or maybe, change the act.

★ 12 ★

CHANGE THE ACT?

"This is not the circus anymore!"

VAUDEVILLE DIES AGAIN!

That was the headline I kept seeing as I was growing up. More vaudeville theaters were dropping the stage show and going to movie-only policies.

The Riggs family had, out of financial necessity, always taken both vaudeville and circus engagements, trying to never have any downtime. When the work moved to fairs, festivals, and nightclubs, we followed the available work. The nightclub business was growing, hiring big bands and variety acts for supper-club stage productions. "Dining, Dancing, and an All-Star Stage Revue" read the ads.

Even though I was in college, I kept calling the agents, looking for employment possibilities. I thought that nightclub revue would be a step up, The New Big Time. Vaudeville and circus were designed for the masses, to attract every class and "children of all ages." Revue would be different. Revue venues served alcohol: children and prudes were banned; we could produce sophisticated entertainment for a sedate, literate audience. Revue was class!

To meet the demands of this new market, The Riggs Brothers would have to change their act.

"Change the act?" Doc responded to that profanity in disbelief.

We had always had some comic patter in the acts, but we were still filling the stage with gymnastic apparatus and The Mighty Magic Trunk. I wanted the new act to be a "suitcase act" that could accept bookings anywhere. A modern act that could be booked on television. By the next year, I was telling agents that we had blended our circus act, our old vaudeville act, and added a fresh "talk" act. The Sacco Agency agreed to list us in their advertising and promised to wire a contract. Now I had to actually produce something that deserved to be called a revue.

But two pantomime clowns do not a revue make.

To live up to our new billing we needed to hire more talent. Doc brought in Paul Bornjorno, our old friend from the World's Fair, a charming "little person," who I remembered mostly because he was so notoriously popular with the ladies. He was built like a prizefighter, with a barrel chest, eighteen-inch biceps, and a high sense of style. It was Paul's talent, charming manner, and easy smile that made him the center of attention, not his forty-two-inch height. Bornjorno did big illusions, such as "The Lady Is Turned into a Tiger," a mostly silent presentation with big fanfare music. But he was at his best when he spoke to the audience, and people forgot his size and felt all the energy he brought to the room.

I said I wanted to hire Marylyn Rice. Doc and Marylyn had been friends for years, though their close friendship had waned. Doc made it clear that I would have to be the one making the job offer. Because I was so keen on building a new act, I would be in charge and responsible for payroll. Doc said, "I do not want to complicate old relationships if your revue idea flops." (Thanks, Dad.)

I was certain that Marylyn, the best all-around female variety talent I had ever met, was perfect casting and not just a woman to stand the act. When she entered the room, it was as if she brought the light. You could not not look at her. She had danced chorus, could do acrobatics, had a trained singing voice, and projected the kind of confidence that most women thought they weren't supposed to have. Marylyn's beauty, taste, and intelligence would make the act.

And, of course, the Bernie Sailor Trio was more than the usual piano, bass, and drums. Fresh out of some Ivy school of music, they could play a wide repertory, classical to popular, but also enjoyed making up calypso songs and limericks from scratch. And they all could double in brass. With nine instruments, the perfect band for a variety revue.

Paul and Doc were a little leery about what Paul called "class differences," and they clearly resented the Trio's educated authority. They were used to the circus, with its "departments" and the top-down pecking order. I wasn't sure we could afford him, but Bernie accepted.

He said that he loved variety but knew that things had to

change. He was very protective of performers' feelings and egos when he took me aside and asked, "How much of this act is cast in stone? I mean, can you change anything without throwing Doc and Paul into apoplexy?"

I said I wasn't familiar with apoplexy. I was worried that Bernie's "new broom" attitude might make things worse, but he gently pressed on.

"Don't you think the audience is smart enough to imagine the setting and furniture just from the voice-over? You don't have to have all those scene sets."

He was right, we were putting a lot of stage time and energy into the setting. "More is sometimes less," he said. He was always saying things like that.

Bernie had suggestions about how to drag our act out from under three generations of Riggs family tradition. Of course, not all of his ideas worked. But that didn't really matter because Doc mellowed and stopped insisting that we only do "what had always worked."

We spent a lot of time talking about old comedy and what Bernie said might be called "new comedy" because it was less joke-dependent. He said that what he had learned in music had given him a greater respect for honesty and spontaneity in comedy.

"Not everything has to be a joke. If you do a good honest character, the audience will give you time to develop the humor truthfully and spontaneously."

"Maybe you should tell Bernie to stick to what he knows and loves," Paul said, knowing that we had all heard his sarcastic remark. I gave him what I thought was a cool-it look.

Marylyn said she admired musicians who could pass musical ideas back and forth, taking and giving, creating new sounds seemingly without a lot of rules or rehearsal.

"That's one of the nice things about jazz. There are no mistakes in jazz. When I make a mistake I play it in; I repeat it and that becomes the new sound. We create new riffs on our mistakes, so I end with no regrets," Bernie said with his best happy face.

Paul was catty. "I, for one, love rehearsal. Missing this rehearsal would have been a big mistake. I would have missed this lecture."

That was the beginning of what became our big makeover.

I started planning the New Riggs Revue. We would offer the acts as a "Crazy House" combination comedy and acrobatic act with our horizontal bar gymnastic act as the second turn. We billed it as Riggs & Riggs and The Crazy Carpenters.

Doc had built what he called The Mighty Magic Trunk, a large steamer trunk on wheels. Props, costumes, wigs, and some fiery stage magic all came from this one black box in the center of the dance floor. Now we could combine circus and vaudeville in the big rooms, but the act wasn't quite right. We added Paul's magic tricks, my juggling, and Marylyn's quick-change "transitions" routine. To support her characters, I added some mock radio bulletins and newspaper commentary, which became my signature shtick. The trunk made the fast move from a "newsroom" to a "bedroom" to an "operating room" or the "flight deck of an airliner" workable. Doc bragged, "Now in the blink of an eye, we can be anywhere!"

I thought that we might be able to create a new sketch, one without a script, working a little Fliffus into the revue, if we could pool our ideas.

"All of us are smarter than any one of us," said Bernie.

"While you pool all of that intelligence, you won't want to read my mind," said Paul.

Doc's vision sounded a lot like the old revue. "They play us in with 'Galloping Comedians.' We flood the stage with acrobatic energy and variety, then we surprise them with our quiet, hopefully thought-provoking, and funny little sketch. Then it fires up again with a shrill whistle blast from Paul as he circles the dance floor on roller skates. He's shouting, 'Extra, Extra, read all about it!' "

(A dwarf on roller skates?)

Paul said, "Ya, me on roller skates! I hand Dudley the paper, very formal, 'Here's tomorrow's news, sir.' Then you start making comments on headlines, but Doc snatches the paper, crosses the stage, and balances it on his nose. Then I roll back by and light it on fire with flash paper. Puff!"

Amid all of this wild, physical movement, quick character impressions, and madcap acrobatics, we'd pause for the sketch, then action erupted again. Doc and Paul said that combining all of these talents showed our versatility and would keep the audience guessing.

An engagement at the Chez Paree in Chicago was set for early summer, with a warm-up date at the Silver Frolics in Calumet City. In the meantime, Doc and Paul were still doing indoor circus dates for Gil Gray. Doc said they were working on props and wardrobe and that they would be ready by our first revue engagement. Their "sight act" pieces and short blackouts were to be woven into the revue lineup when they returned. They were working only on the traditional variety bits. "The ones that always work," said Doc.

I thought I could get a head start working on Fliffus ideas.

Working with Bernie and Marylyn forced me to finally grow up. I was now the youngest member of the ensemble but expected to lead these seasoned performers through an untested production. I worked hard to maintain my excitement as we went into rehearsals, but I worried that I might be out of my depth.

★ 13 ★

YES . . . PLEASE!

"Comedy is based on negation," said Paul.
"No. Comedy is based on truth," countered Bernie.
"Comedy is based on timing," I said.

Nothing from my past qualified me for this.

The circus had rules, I was used to rules. The circus has a hierarchy that dictates clear instructions and expects that all orders will be followed exactly. The traditional circus is successful only because each of the departments has a person in charge who makes that department succeed. And all of the many departments come together to forge a successful, entertaining performance under the direction of the ringmaster.

I told everyone to come to rehearsal with at least ten new ideas. "Everything that you think should be included in a big-time nightclub revue."

Doc, Paul, Marylyn, and I were from the circus. Bernie came from jazz. I'd added Robin Mack and Don Engels, "kids"—though they were probably just a few years older than I—from the local student theater crowd. All show-business people. People "with it" enough to know what was expected. I said, "This is a group think rehearsal. Just shout it out."

Everybody was smiling but nobody spoke. I said, "Don't be shy!"

Marylyn began to explain her idea for a scene and got quickly interrupted. Don was laughing at her. This happened a few more times before she lost her smile. Nothing at that moment was funny or even pleasant, so she just stopped. "What's the use? This is not the circus. This thing of yours won't work as a top-down system."

That got my attention.

I was embarrassed. I thought, "I'm in charge! Why am I feeling like a schmuck?" I walked away, talking to myself (quietly) . . . "I hire smart, talented people. I hire them to be creative, then I kill their creativity? If I want their talent and ideas, I have to give *them* control, not some control, real control. To be the boss, in fact 'I can't be the boss.'"

Circus tradition got eighty-sixed in the middle of my first rehearsal.

I rolled out the blackboard and reminded the performers that I had asked them to show up today with ideas.

"The goal of today is to collect ideas. Not to judge ideas. We need lots and lots of ideas. All ideas, even crazy things, improper things, nasty things. Ideas you can't tell your mother. Nothing censored, everything gained."

Marylyn wrote down some of what I had just said and kept

adding comments. Problem was, no one was listening or connecting to each other. Then came individual monologues. Each performer glommed onto an idea from the board, made some funny remarks, and erased the item. It was like sitting through an hour of auditions.

Bernie and I did a demonstration of Word Jazz as a warm-up for Don and Robin, the new kids. They giggled. "Now *we're* auditioning for them?" Bernie smiled.

Don suggested "passing the talking stick," something he learned in the Boy Scouts. Bernie liked cueing the next speaker by a touch, but that had a halting stop–go rhythm and wouldn't work across a stage.

"We know two-person riffing works . . . sometimes. But when you get everybody talking at once, interrupting, not knowing when to speak, it's just a waste of time. Can we work on something else?" said Bernie.

"Maybe we need a conductor . . . or a traffic cop," I said.

Marylyn laughed that great infectious laugh and said, "Let us think more . . . simply. We have a problem: how to control stop and go?" She paused, then said, "A visa, permission, a tollgate. No. A gatekeeper! And a password. Maybe all you need is a password."

"Like what?" asked Bernie. "Halt! Who goes there?"

"Like a simple, polite 'Please' or perhaps 'Yes.'" She was smiling as she warmed to the idea. "After all, who are we? We are, if I do say so myself, five nice decent people. We usually listen to each other, we don't often quibble . . . much. We're civilized, trusting friends with a common goal of creating and telling an original story to our audience. Simple courtesy should allow us to do that!" Marylyn gestured to the right—"Please let me in." Then to the left—"Yes, of course."

Was that it? Could it be that simple? We started over. "Please" and "Yes" would serve as passwords and replace the touch tag for cues.

I wrote on the board: "Friendly, courteous manners, attentive listening, and polite requests allow freely associated ideas/words to become dialogue." That looked good, but too pretentiously academic and certainly not complete. I knew the definition of what we were trying to do would continue to grow. I suggested, "Don't be shy, enter into the action verbally. The touch tag way of cueing just changes the focus to someone else. You can't just pass it like a ball, you need to stop, and talk to each other, create a dialogue."

Everyone said, "I know, I know."

I'd had enough. I blew the whistle (circus talk). "I don't like rules, but we need a traffic cop." So I made some rules:

Don't use "I know" as a comma.

Don't hog the scene.

Be kind to each other. Always be courteous.

Please use "Please" as your password to enter a scene.

If you are the gatekeeper, please accept "Please" and let someone enter the scene.

The sometimes-shy Robin added "judgment," "trust," "respect" to the board. We made a circle again and started practicing quick word exchanges. Everyone was having fun, enjoying the process of spontaneously making up a scene. It was still confusing, but the flow got smoother, the words got smarter as we went to full sentences, some of which actually made sense.

Today, this all sounds a little too pat. I don't remember it being quite that simple. But I do know that when we tried "Yes," to acknowledge, and "Please," to continue, something close to dialogue began to flow. Questions and interruptions with new information merged without stopping the scene. Word Jazz went from single-word exchanges to whole meaningful sentences and began to sound a lot like normal conversation.

After all of my overthinking, the key to Fliffus was common courtesy, even if the scene was raucous.

Sometimes you can see something only after you stop looking. Marylyn had taught us manners, and that changed attitudes. *Mutual respect unlocked people's talents.* With the more relaxed, confident state of mind, the ensemble started to develop and the work got better. Slowly.

But still I did not want to give up the insurance provided by the sight gags. I was still the boss but was keeping that a secret.

The Fliffus evolved and grew other dimensions, and as it made more sense, it started to be fun. It went into the middle of our nightclub revue act, next to my newspaper bit. One by one, the sight gags were replaced with words. Surprise laughter from audience insight began to seem better than pratfalls.

Today, the process, the method, others might even say the religion, is practiced everywhere. Improvisation is studied and debated endlessly. For some it has become a way of life. For me, it was always a tool for entertainment.

But it didn't work for everyone, and it didn't work overnight. In fact, everything changed for us in the summer of 1953, not long after we had figured out the Fliffus.

What I remember as "The Fliffus Fuss" occurred when Marylyn Rice tried to teach Paul Bornjorno to simply say "yes." I was surprised that saying "yes" to Marylyn could be a problem for anyone, but Paul did not want "some new untried idea" to corrupt our long-established family vaudeville act.

We had been getting a few good-paying Chicago club dates, but it was spotty work with no predictable cash flow. I had already spent my tuition money, reworking the act, trusting Tommy Sacco to come through on his promise of steady New York nightclub employment. Waiting for Sacco to book that work had made our nerves a little raw.

I knew we had to dump some bits that had been in the act forever. I wanted to add "The Fliffus" in the middle of our routine and transform our "sight act" into a "talk act." After years of success doing pantomime comedy, Paul was not eager to change. "We have to keep what always works." Doc thought that the sight gags should stay in the act. "You might need a pratfall to rescue the act if all your words fail you."

I couldn't know if he was just being loyal to tradition or to Paul.

Paul's usually reliable energy had been replaced by a sour petulance. When I was hiring, I asked Paul what he thought of Marylyn. "She is way too smart for me." Coming from a man known for his love of women, that didn't quite jibe.

I had also asked Marylyn what she thought of Bornjorno. "He always makes me think happy thoughts," she said with a little giggle.

They seemed to get along, but there was something, an edge. Thanks to Bernie and his happy piano, I figured that the edge would fade away. I assumed that Marylyn, a woman with whom everyone falls in love, should be able to charm Paul into trying something new.

"With the Fliffus, we listen to each other to keep the idea moving. We set a mood and try to make it better. Always say 'yes,' when you receive a line, then add your own true idea to it." Marylyn gingerly repeated the basic points of the method, stressing that the passwords, "please" and "yes," be used to enable dialogue and replace the old gag-loaded monologues we grew up performing.

Paul was not going to be a willing student, so we had some unexpected drama. Doc said, "This may be more trouble than it's worth, Son. They will either fall in love or murder each other; either way we lose them. And we can't afford to lose Paul."

I looked at him, face on, and said, "And what about Marylyn, Dad?"

Marylyn, always sunny and upbeat said, "Can you just try it? You might like it."

Paul said, "NO, THANK YOU."

"I thought we were all adults here. Why can't you just say 'yes'? You're so great at saying 'no.' Why? Why can't you men just say 'yes' "?

Paul riled, "Because you women manage to always say 'no' to the men who say 'yes.'"

She tried reasoning. "Every time you go for the joke, the scene stops."

Paul sputtered, "I don't need you to tell me what will get a laugh. What do you know about being funny for money?" he scorned. "Because 'no' is funny. 'Yes' is not funny!" He was gathering his stuff, getting ready to walk out. "All of this high-hat truth and courtesy crap is not getting us an act. You have to have a finish, a punch line to get off stage."

Marylyn said, "A finish will evolve if you just let it happen."

"Yes, but . . ." Paul was running out of negatives.

"When you say 'Yes, but,' it's the same as 'No.' You reject the idea. Try to be positive, nix the negation," said Marylyn.

(That set him off.)

"Comedy is based on negation!"

Bernie spoke up. "No. Comedy is based on truth."

I said, "Comedy is based on timing," trying to make peace.

"Laugh at me . . . but I was hoping that comedy could be based on cooperation. I thought we just might be smart enough to build on Word Jazz and create something new."

Marylyn never gave up on Paul, but I had to. All that fuss during rehearsal remains in my memory as a kind of revelatory moment. A Riggs family pivot point. Family tradition gave way, and our variety sight act became a talk act. But Doc and Paul went back to indoor circus dates, taking The Mighty Magic Trunk with them.

After Paul and Doc left us in Chicago, we became more confident as a talk act but still held on to a few visual bits we thought the audience expected. The audience response to the first pratfall of the evening provided an education about that evening's crowd. We were transforming the act each time we played. "We have to teach the audience what to expect," said Bernie.

Working the Kansas City clubs, we had learned to expect some rude, often raw participation from audiences that sometimes enjoyed their drinks more than our entertainment. "What kinda act is this?" a patron asked in a voice that confirmed what I could smell. Don, in his toughest voice, challenged the guy with, "Who do you hate?" That broke the ice with the audience, and they provided five or six names to work into the scene. ("Nixon" and "McCarthy" were offered at almost every show.) The talk part of the act always worked better at the early show, before the audience got too "tired."

I knew we could manage the late shows by asking, "Who do you love?," and I could also garner ideas from the sober part of the audience by quoting fresh news items from the newspaper and asking, "What do you think about that?"

My parents had introduced me to "Who do you love?" "Who do you hate?"—the stage technique they originated to control vaudeville hecklers and nightclub drunks. The Humanettes used audience suggestions as material for the always spontaneous set. My folks would never have said that their act was "improvisational theater," but the act established a tradition of encouraging and valuing audience involvement.

In presenting Word Jazz, we were a lot like The Humanettes, captive to the stage and expected to perform something "interesting" on the spot. Don and Robin learned to grab the focus with their handshake gag, a distraction that allowed Marylyn a moment of thought, as she began Roun-delay, tossing out the first word. That first word had to rotate back and be my last word to finish the set. Then Robin would step back in and reprise the opening sight gag.

The money was good. We were getting some work.

We were getting better at something, but I wasn't sure that it was the right something. Certainly not the cool club act that I thought could headline at the Palmer House or Radio City. We headed to New York City for the Sacco bookings. We were ready. I hoped.

★ 14 ★

INSTANT THEATER

"Somebody likes us!"

The day before Halloween, when our agent Tommy Sacco closed his New York office and went back to Chicago, he left us unexpectedly "at liberty." Twenty-four weeks of East Coast bookings, which were to provide half our livelihood, were gone. There would be no paycheck until the circus opened again in April.

Overnight, our job security was shattered. The long-held, almost gospel belief that a talented vaudeville performer could enjoy endless employment was likewise shattered. Veteran performers who had built successful vaudeville careers working for the agency were in shock. We had been getting club work in Chicago and Kansas City, but now I wanted to succeed in New York again. I had invested my tuition money in developing the revue, but now the promised East Coast bookings had vanished.

Sacco had booked us for just one engagement before he folded. "That was a long drive for one gig," Bernie said. With no cash flow, I knew that my plan for revue and TV was screeching to a halt, stranding everyone who had worked so hard to make the new act work.

Several other acts lingered in the hall outside Sacco's office, unable to give up on the hope that the often playful Tommy would show up and say, "Just kidding, folks." No one came, except a man who replaced the fancy gold leaf "Variety Agency" sign with cold black letters that said "Space Available."

Robin said, "That's us, available."

I felt a sick, empty frustration, knowing that my big-shot plan had changed without my consent. Through the glass panel on Sacco's abandoned door I could read the sign he had left behind. It said, "You are not in show business if you are laying off." Sacco had used that sign as both a threat and a promise. No act wants to lay off; in my family, it would have been a disgrace to say, "I had to go on relief." Besides, the unemployment office doesn't list jobs for acrobats, jugglers, or clowns.

Everyone was talking all at once, working toward a collective group panic. The always happy-faced Bernie Sailor said, "What about doing some showcase shows? We can get the other agents in to see the acts, get us a few dates to tide us over. You know, an invited audition." The very next day, Paul Bornjorno came out of the past and to the rescue. "Move your stuff over here. I've rented a rehearsal hall at 50th and Broadway. I've got Ken Murray coming to see us as soon as we have something to sell." Paul was his old happy self, showing

149

none of the stubborn sourness that got him eighty-sixed from our Chicago club act.

A week later, the Bernie Sailor Trio—piano, bass, and drums, with doubling on trumpet, sax, and trombone—played an overture at 8:30 p.m. sharp, and we did our first rag-a-tag showcase show to an audience of seven off-duty waiters.

Thankfully, there was applause to quell our "Why am I in show business?" blues. Some happy clapping was coming from the off-duty restaurant help, and through the open windows we could hear people on the sidewalk chattering about "something was going on" upstairs. Bernie's sweet music glommed onto the passing pedestrians. Most New Yorkers walked on by, but some paused, stood, even applauded before going on their way. "It's just like working the crowd in Union Square but without the tip jar," said Robin.

Paul moved the stage area up tight to the windows and told us to "sell to the gawkers, and make it interesting!"

The few people watching from the sidewalk attracted a small crowd, which drew a larger crowd, and soon people were trying to enter the unmarked stairway door.

"Somebody likes us!" said Marylyn, waving out the window.

After being surprised and hurt by Sacco, we were starving for anything that might restore our confidence. Feeling wanted, even by people on the other side of the street, raised morale and made us feel like we were still in what Doc always called "the business of entertaining the show-going public."

A coffee company restaurant chain was introducing instant coffee, a new product, on big posters and oilcloth banners. Paul swiped some of the banners and painted their trademark checkerboard background, leaving only the word *Instant*. The word *Theater* was then added in six-inch-high, bold Barnum letters that declared our rehearsal hall was now the Instant Theater, with performances at 8:30, tickets at the door.

The program changed at every show, an hour and a half of variety, utilizing unemployed acts: a vocal quartet, roller-skating acrobatics, ballroom dancing, a unicyclist, a magician, and us.

The highlight of the nightclub act we did at the Instant Theater used audience suggestions to create short comedy sketches on the spot, all based on "Who do you love? Who do you hate?" and my news items from the newspaper. Nobody expected a talk act in the middle of a slapstick acrobatic sight act. "In confusion, there may be profit," I said hopefully. Bernie's trio invented music under our made-up, on-the-spot lyrics and provided mood music to support the sketches. Bernie's improvised jazz riffs were perfect to set up the bit we called "Word Jazz." We were improvising comedy to improvised music in a live, unrehearsed theater production. Using audience-suggested words, Marylyn, Robin, Don, and I created short, usually, and, we hoped, funny sketches on the spot.

The clubs were hard work but predictable money. Now we were essentially busking in a rehearsal hall to unpredictable money, but we were having fun.

The Instant Theater was the first adult job I ever had that was free of the Riggs family banner and that was not dependent on sight gags and pantomime. Doc always said that he hated college towns because the audience was too smart for broad slapstick comedy. Now I found myself re-working a dumb-act show production in a smart-show town.

Paul Bornjorno made me a gift of the lease. "Don't thank me. And don't sue me if this thing flops," he said when he and Doc left for Canada to join the circus. My father's parting words were "Wire me if you need money."

I was leaving circus and variety show business for satire, even though Fred Allen had long since declared "Satire is what closes on Saturday night." I wanted desperately to prove that he was wrong. I had convinced myself that the Instant Theater show would be a hit! And for a few days, it drew an audience that fed our hunger for applause. But there was no money to advertise, so the people who came attended almost by acci-dent. The show got better, but smaller, as acts found other work and left. Then the landlord clued me in on the fact that the space was "not in legal compliance." He kept taking rent, but I knew.

Robin suggested that we take the Instant Theater on tour. It seemed like the next great idea. Well, maybe not. Bernie intro-duced me to Thom Broadbent, his old concert agent, who was in the music-recording business. Broadbent said that the best audience for Word Jazz would be college students who buy novelty recordings. He offered fixed-fee concert contracts to campus bookers in Boston, Washington, Atlanta, Saint Louis, Chicago, and ending in Minneapolis. "A few college engage-ments will be a good way for me to test your act. See if it sells, and see if you have legs," Broadbent said. (No one had noticed that these colleges would not start classes until after we had performed there.)

With seven people crowded into an unreliable station wagon, our Grand Tour took a loop down the East Coast and back up through Chicago, seven cities in twenty-one days. Bernie's sidemen quit after Chicago.

When we got to Minneapolis, the agent had lost the contract, moved us into another venue, and all that running around forced a very late curtain and a restless audience.

But the show still worked. Losing two-thirds of the band may have been a blessing. Four actors plus piano (smaller than the advertised seven) actually worked better, was more portable, and felt more like a family. We were doing better, were more confident, had more intentional work. Onstage, my little, thrown-together troupe acted as if they had years of experience, happily enjoying performance and applause. Offstage, we rarely stopped rehearsing, constantly exercising, testing new ideas, and encouraging each other. Robin said, "All this warm trust and devotion reminds me of immersion Bible camp."

It was all about trust. Trusting yourself onstage and knowing that your partners will protect you if you make a mistake are very liberating. Our friendships grew on the road; Marylyn and Bernie were always close, Don and Robin acted like siblings; we made a point of always being civil to each other. As we became better performers, Fliffus had made us into an ensemble of better, more caring humans.

But then it was over.

The Instant Theater tour was *not* a huge commercial success. The show had tightened up and was usually well received once the audience got past their confused expectations. But we went broke anyway.

Even though a newspaper review said, "The Instant Theater performance: Showed great promise," my dream of improvisational success faded as I thought about the future. I was again at liberty.

Don and Robin went seeking some better-paying activities. Bernie and Marylyn, as usual, bounced right back to work. They took a hotel piano-bar gig, singing at a place called the Norsk Room. I knew that the Shrine Circus would open in spring. But I could no longer ignore the uncertainty of show-business bookings. I thought that if I got my degree I might be able to teach school, even from a wheelchair should I fall again. My health was good, and I had healed up pretty well—but I could not deny the hazards. I was forced to admit that, despite my billing, I was no longer the undisputed King of the Air.

I signed up for a dozen credits at the University of Minnesota in Minneapolis.

I joined my new university classmates, mostly theater majors, who were well ahead of me academically and who could not care less about my background. My adviser couldn't understand why at my age I was still an undergrad. All my family's show-business history didn't mean a thing, so I avoided answering questions about my past. I knew I would be going out on the road again when paying work was available, and leaving was not something that would endear me with students and faculty, though some faculty would certainly be happy to see me gone.

As luck would have it, I got booked for a series of TV shows in Chicago. But the back-and-forth between show commitments and college classes began upsetting people. The WGN director in Chicago worried that my weekly commute between Chicago and Minneapolis was cutting time too thin. "If you got so much as a flat tire, you'll miss rehearsal and then where will *I* be?"

These engagements paid well, but the travel time erased study time and much of the profit. Driving to Chicago on Friday, rehearsing Saturday morning, doing the show Saturday, then driving the four hundred miles back to Minneapolis on Sunday didn't really leave me in prime shape for class on Monday.

The head of the theater department couldn't understand why I refused a nonspeaking role in *Oedipus* during this time. "Theater students are expected to participate in school productions. You must make yourself available weekends," read the backstage posted notice.

I explained again that I was classified "working student" and my television contract required my presence in Chicago every weekend.

He said he was not going to waste his time on my problems. "You need to decide if you really want to continue in this department." It was definitely *his department.* He ruled with religiously warm manners, clear rules, and a sweet cheerfulness. He was held in highest regard by just about everyone. I was out of line. I came here to *study* stage direction, and I was not taking direction.

"I need you in the crowd scene," he said softly.

I knew I was not making things better when I said, "It would be hard for me to quit a paying job in show business to carry a spear in one scene of an amateur college play." I should not have used "amateur." He stood up, and smilingly ushered me out of his office saying, "Again, I think you must decide if you really want to stay in theater."

Twenty-five years later, he wrote about improvisation and the Brave New Workshop Theater in his history of Minnesota theater:

In the good old days when a drugstore sold drugs and a service station sold gasoline, when a Ford was a Ford and a Buick a Buick, vaudeville was vaudeville, opera was opera and the legitimate theater legitimate—a place where properly written plays were memorized by actors for presentation before an audience. That has passed. Today drugstores and service stations sell everything from playing cards to Bibles. Fords and Buicks sell everything from luxury limousines to cramped compacts, and so the legitimate theater also tries to be all things to all people, hesitating not a moment to steal from ballet, variety, burlesque, opera or whatever. Consequently, we can no longer eliminate Dudley Riggs from this book, even though his productions are probably no more "legitimate" than were those of Buffalo Bill or Weber and Fields back in the good old days. (From *Minnesota Theatre* by Professor Frank M. Whiting, Director of the University of Minnesota Theatre)

Thank you, Dr. Whiting, for the kind thought.

———•———

In those days, I neverthless kept in touch with the agents. I couldn't seem to stop looking for work. And occasionally they would come through with a short-run contract.

One memorable Saturday, after the early Shrine Circus matinee in Minneapolis, a small group waited with program and autograph books in hand, eager to give the usual compliments and thanks to the performers. These were real circus fans, always the ideal audience, folks who obviously loved circus and the idea of meeting, of knowing, even briefly, someone in the circus. "If they stayed after, they must have liked the show. Getting backstage is not easy, so they must really want to meet you," said Dubb Harden. These children were all so giggly and shy, so full of compliments, how could I not get puffed up. I loved them for loving me.

It *had* been a great performance, considering the early hour. I had added a new move in the sway pole act, making the descent look a lot riskier, and building to a more dynamic finale. I did it for the adults, for the dating couples, setting up an unexpected moment that would cause them to gasp and then hold each other a little tighter. It wasn't for the children. I figured that the kids would be distracted by the cotton candy salesman.

After this particular matinee, a tall, beautiful woman dressed in a black leather trench coat waited patiently until the family crowd had moved on, then surprised me with "I waited to talk to you because I didn't want to rob you of the children's sweet little parade of well-wishing." I was set back thinking, *She's a little sarcastic, rather too direct, but well spoken. Why all that fire in her eyes?* This woman was riled up about something! Could she be angry at me? For what? Looking me directly in the eye and standing just a bit too close, she said, "You should be ashamed of yourself!"

When a lone woman comes backstage, she usually brings flowers and some nice but empty town girl chatter. I confess, I really didn't mind the giggly chatter—it occasionally led to a real talk—once the backstage fright wore off. After our initial nervous jousting, when the words slowed down, and some personality emerged, it was then possible to have a real conversation.

Not this time. This lady lit into me as if I had caused a car crash.

"You should be ashamed of yourself, setting such a bad example for these children," she continued. "You make reckless behavior look like fun. Don't you know that if kids try that, they are sure to get hurt! Stop that!"

Wow! I had grown used to hearing nothing but praise for my performance. *What a gutsy woman,* I thought. *She put it right out there, no concession offered, just an unequivocal "Stop doing that!"* She walked away a few steps, and then stopped, and said, "Think about what you are doing, Riggs!"

She was gone before I could ask how she happened to use my real name. The program only listed me as "The Great Alberty."

Two years later our paths crossed again in Minneapolis where I was once more enrolled in college. Vaudeville was dead, concession salesmen were obscuring the art of the circus, and I had no bookings for Word Jazz. The Instant Theater had proved that Fliffus was a useful tool for creating new comedy, but Word Jazz hadn't generated enough interest to support itself anywhere except New York.

I managed to stay unpacked and off the road for almost a full college year. I had moved so often that I had no idea where home might be. I had been a kid posing as an adult for so long. Now I realized that I had never quite grown up.

When she and I finally met formally, I immediately realized that I had seen her before—two years back at the Shrine Circus. When it came time for introductions, she brushed right past any kind of protocol.

"Hi. We've met before. I'm Ruth. I'm a PK—a preacher's kid, I'm on the dean's list, I edit the college literary magazine, and I make great Indian curry," she said all in one breath.

I had to step back and catch *my* breath. *Could it be that this attractive, refreshingly direct woman is asking me home for a curry dinner?* I wondered? "Well, hello," I stammered.

She made no room for the usual small talk. She *was* asking me out, and I soon discovered she did cook great curry.

I had seen her on campus and always had a nagging thought that I had met her someplace before. She stood out, always dressed away from the standard skirt, sweater, and bobby socks uniform. There was nothing standard about this woman. She had an unusually elegant way of holding herself—not haughty, but very self-assured. I soon learned that she was a classical pianist, a poet, and an outspoken social radical. She laughed easily and seemed forever surrounded by her egghead friends. I had kept my distance, unwilling to risk being on the wrong side of that easy, sarcastic laugh. Of course, we became friends.

In the spring, I was about to leave the university again. I had a contract that would keep me on the road and out of school for six months.

"Why not stay and finish and maybe have more choices?" Ruth asked.

"I have to make a living! I have a contract," I responded, though deep down I knew she was right. "We have a family tradition of always honoring our contracts."

Ruth looked me straight in the eye and with a very knowing smile said, "Is that family tradition or just a rationalization that you live by?" (I was hearing an echo of what Marylyn Rice had said to me.) "You *can* do other jobs, you know. Maybe you should unload some of your circus baggage and give school a chance."

It was 1956. I stayed in school, maried Ruth, opened a coffeehouse, and ran Instant Theater, which eventually became Dudley Riggs' Brave New Workshop. I didn't leave show business, but I *did* run away from the circus.

★ 15 ★

THE NEW IDEAS
PROGRAM

Ad lib—ad absurdum.

In the circus, we lived one thing after another, "upping and downing" the circus big top in a new town every day. We would arrive . . . set it up, perform the show, repeat it, sometimes with surprises and catastrophes. But always fun. The uncertainty is why it was fun. Perhaps I'd learned not to make plans because so many plans failed. It's like a flying act when routines are learned through failure in order to be safe. Many flyers train by learning every "trick to the net"—do the trick, but miss the catch and learn to recover by going to the net. To echo what I told new recruits to the circus: "A failed trick in rehearsal gives you the confidence to complete the trick in performance."

In my late twenties, I was still trying to figure out what it was that I wanted to do when I grew up. (I've continued to do that all these years.) I was wondering, "Who am I this week?" As Grandmother Riggs said, "Show business is ephemeral. Work goes away." Well, my work had gone away again.

I'd gone from The Riggs Brothers circus act to my Instant Theater; great for a while, but it didn't pay the bills. I said, "Let's tour it!" The tour only proved that the best audience for Instant Theater was probably college students, but I still went broke. To earn some money, I then joined another circus mid-season, but they didn't need my act; I was reduced to selling balloons.

I had run out of touring jobs and needed to just stay in one place and rethink my life. Go home. But where? I realized that I had never thought that I had a hometown. Now I thought I should try to be a settled resident and become known as a "towner" to my circus friends and relatives.

In our show-business life, whenever my family was booked into a new city, we followed a family ritual. We'd ask each other, "What does this town need?" Taking turns around the table, each of us would declare what each town we found ourselves in needed to be a better place:

. . . you could buy chicory-free coffee in New Orleans.

. . . L.A. would have a kosher deli.

. . . there would be opera in Tulsa.

. . . bread that was not sourdough would be available in San Francisco.

When I came back to Minneapolis and married Ruth, I had decided to stay put. And my answer to what this town needed was good bread, espresso, and satire.

In 1956, Stefano's Pizza—a tiny atmospheric café on Cedar Avenue near the university—became the new home for Word Jazz, the Instant Theater, and the New Ideas Program. These titles seemed grandiose, but less so when set in the humble storefront with its all-jazz jukebox and low lighting. A sign over the door read, "Pizza, Jazz and Thou." I was half expecting flack from local scribes or from people I had known at the university who might have been inclined to ask, "Who do you think you are and what qualifies you to talk about new ideas?" But, to my surprise, no one challenged it. People seemed to think it was cool. Such were the times.

As a newly married man, I needed to be a civilian, act like a regular adult, and find a suitable job. Most of what I had learned on the road and at the university so far failed to qualify me for employment in the regular workforce. I knew I would have to create my own job. I needed to establish a home base, create something new, do some shows, make some noise, have some fun, and bring people together. Maybe even generate some of what I, in my callow wisdom, thought this town needed.

Stefano's was only the second pizzeria to open in the Twin Cities, and it stayed open until 2 a.m. Pretty exotic for a city not yet known for its nightlife. In the 1950s, Minneapolis was a very quiet community. Late-night entertainment options in Minneapolis and St. Paul were few, and the very idea of late-night *live* entertainment was branded sinful by most. Bernie introduced me to Tony, the charming Italian owner, saying, "You guys need each other."

I signed a lease for Stefano's and produced the first late-night poetry and jazz concert. Nice crowd, mostly curiosity-driven, but they had a good time, and I promised more to come. No one knew what to expect from this shoestring enterprise, so "more to come" almost sounded like a joke. That may have been part of its charm.

"Free entertainment at midnight" became popular with the audience and with the musicians, most of whom had paying jobs elsewhere. At Stefano's there was no booze, no curfew, so jazz riffing and theater works in progress often ran late. Musicians became protective of the place, and we maintained a nearly Sunday school behavior code to help me ward off any activity that might put my license at risk. Troublesome un-hip types were cut from the clan. The mood was free and easy, but with rules, so that artists could stay focused on their art.

Stefano's served as a magnet for artists, musicians, and a few experienced student actors who found that they tired of only being cast in community or church basement stage productions. Such were the times. When I came to town, there were seven theaters and six critics. The Guthrie Theater would not arrive until 1963.

"Instant Theater presents The New Ideas Program" came to mean a potpourri of staged readings of new plays such as *The Bald Soprano* or *In-Visible,* Beat poets such as Ferlinghetti and Ginsberg read to jazz, chamber music quartets, and modern dance. Adding poetry and modern dance helped create the "something new" I had promised myself that I wanted to offer along with entertainment and surprise, thoughtful surprise. And I hoped the audience would give us a thoughtful reaction and regular attendance.

I cast a dozen actors in a few productions of new and locally unseen works—Baraka, Ionesco, Beckett—each lightly produced in a Reader's Theater format. Some actors came to the first rehearsal excited but dubious about the neighborhood and the unfamiliar scripts. The young women worried that appearing onstage at Stefano's might harm their reputation; the guys thought it would help theirs. Yes, such were the times.

We began to conclude each evening's performance with midnight Word Jazz. The audience was growing, seemed older and more receptive to fresh sounds and ideas, just more hip. Actors from the university were interested but restricted by the late hours and fear of offending their theater professors. I kept trying to introduce actors to the Fliffus concept, but I took criticism from the university theater department, which claimed we were being disrespectful to the power of the playwright because "they just make up the script!"

I printed off the first issue of *The Broadside*, the "official newsletter" of The New Ideas Program. Money was short, and this was to be our only paid-for advertising. We proudly papered all the dorms. Attendance grew. We sent it to Will Jones and Don Morrison at the daily papers, and they would occasionally pick up on our events. We had no other way to announce our existence or our programs because we were not part of the tightly established theater community. We mailed a few broadsides to names on the progressive Walker Art Center members list. Attendance grew. But we also received three letters from Walker members requesting that their names be removed from the Instant Theater's mailing list.

I also posted flyers advertising a Fliffus workshop for actors:

FLIFFUS:

An ongoing effort to expand the acceptance of free association speech by theater artists and audience.

A workshop to introduce free-flowing ideas.

An actor's exercise to try to create original scenes through free association.

At the first session, I gave eight actors audition scripts to read through, then asked them to run the first scene. Most stage-wise actors can perform easily when they have the authority provided by a physical script. With pages in hand, even from an unfamiliar or discredited work, they can move convincingly about the stage and respond to cues, in character and with some conviction.

Then I took away their scripts. "Please do the scene again without the script. You know the plot; you know your characters. Now do the scene again the best you can, with your imagination engaged. Keep the characters and the cues, but make new dialogue from the words that come first to your mind. Make it up as you go along.

"Don't worry about the right words. These are the right words because they are your words. They are free, honest words because they come from what you and your character know at this moment in time. Keep an open mind."

The workshops were successful in gathering together talented freethinkers, actors, artists, and writers who wanted to be a part of something new. After a while, the actors began to trust themselves, trust their talent. They started to trust me. They started to bloom.

Youthful energy prevailed. Signs were posted backstage—thoughtful shibboleths that defined how the actors viewed the process and their art:

We are free to fail, but we are free to do anything.

Free to do what others are afraid to do.

Free to do really outstanding work.

We can do anything!

Trust, honesty, and freedom unlock the artist to be great.

These were hip kids—they got it. And so it grew.

Eventually, we got to the point where the actors were simply given the idea of a scene with an interesting theme—for example, "newly married couple entertaining in-laws." Onstage, the actors each added ideas, created small talk, and the scene became richer, building toward something interesting.

After a year at Stefano's, it was time to put ourselves under our own roof. I wanted to create a coffeehouse with the elegant atmosphere of places I had seen in Vienna. We searched for a location: we wanted an "interesting-looking" building with two rooms that could be both a café and a theater available at a low rent. We drove around looking for a building that was interesting—not necessarily one that was appropriate—and found an old radiator repair shop a little farther east from campus on University Avenue. This would become the Café Espresso.

When my father and I had left Europe after our circus engagement had ended, we had had a fair amount of money, but had been told we weren't allowed to bring British currency into the United States. So our feeling was that we better spend it. My father invested in small, lightweight, easily fungible cameras. I bought a rack of Penguin books that weren't available in the States (my copy of Henry Miller's banned book *Tropic of Cancer* was confiscated at customs) and a very heavy copper La Pavoni espresso machine. My Grandmother Riggs had introduced me to rich espresso coffee when I was eight by taking me to a coffeehouse called Caffé Reggio in Greenwich Village (it is still there). And so it was that eighteen years after visiting Reggio's for the first time, I brought the first espresso machine to Minnesota.

We painted the walls a deep royal red, hung heavy gold brocade drapes that had been rescued from the Radio City Theater, displayed copies of Rembrandt paintings in gold frames, and put "Café Espresso" in gold leaf on the front door. At Stefano's we had offered an all-jazz jukebox, but here we played only classical music. Through an early customer, I found a marvelous woman, a Hungarian immigrant, who offered to make Sacher torte. And I had to learn how to bake my own "salt and pepper" bread for the one sandwich we offered: a European ham and cheese with good mustard.

"Nordeast" is one of the liveliest parts of the city now. But in the late 1950s it was a rough neighborhood with hard-drinking bars, church missions, Scientologists, and the Socialist Workers Party headquarters down the block from us. We were not welcomed by local merchants, who were inclined to believe that anyone selling espresso had to be a beatnik. Customers were outraged by espresso cappuccino at fifty cents a cup. Business was slow. But because of bridge construction over the Mississippi, symphony-goers on their way to see the Minneapolis Symphony Orchestra at Northrop Auditorium had to go right by our front door. Thankfully, Café Espresso became popular with people of artistic taste.

All the same, Café Espresso was started with three strikes already against us: an espresso place with Viennese decor in 1957 Minneapolis, a new kind of entertainment based in satire and audience participation, and a restaurant being run by two people with no previous business experience.

When the Café Espresso building was sold two years later for urban renewal, that eviction landed us around the corner at 207 East Hennepin. We did the move with help from our loyal clientele. Regular espresso drinkers volunteered to hand-carry the entire contents of the café the two blocks to Hennepin. But now we had no parking lot. During the first three years at Café Espresso, our income went up; we moved around the corner, and it went right back down.

East Hennepin was the first time we had my name over the door. The building had been a beauty parlor, and one of the reasons they probably went out of business was that they'd invested in a huge sign—an eight-foot-high, two-sided panel. Richard Guindon, a coconspirator who later became a syndicated cartoonist, took on the job of painting a new sign; he completed "Coffee House" on one side of it and then asked the question: What are we going to put on the other side? This was the first time my name was part of our operation: Dudley Riggs' Café Espresso.

We kept the same menu, music, and feel, but now we had no back room. Up front, there was a bar with our coffee machine and café, and at the other end we used two platforms on one side and another in front of the piano on the other. The question was: How do you create a backstage? Some wanted curtains, but I thought we ought to use three revolving doors, the backdrop I had used performing in vaudeville as part of The Crazy Carpenters.

The two stages and three doors, which became our trademark, allowed us to make the quick entrances and exits needed for blackouts. I liked being able to get one or two thoughtful sentences from one actor, but made funny by the suddenness of another actor's entrance. Surprise moments to create an unpredictable rhythm to the revue.

When the audience already knows where the scene is going to go, a blackout allows us to start something else, then come back and finish that scene. You're smartening up the audience to accept the cutaway scene—say, insert a scene from *Oedipus* in the middle of another sketch. Tiresias appears and speaks a line from a Greek tragedy that adds substance to the comedy sketch. Make the audience think "Where did that come from?" I think we must constantly be ready to surprise the audience with something new, even if unrelated or illogical. Virtually every actor I've worked with had something they would love to say onstage, even though it had nothing to do with the show.

At the same time, I didn't want the café to be labeled as a beatnik coffee shop. What combination could I live with to stay in business but still produce Instant Theater and develop Fliffus? We tried it all. It was a time of constant serendipity, new people, and new chemistry. It was of a time of "Let's just see if it works." We had a poet who was quite brilliant at reading poetry accompanied by a jazz trio. Someone would come forward with a new play they'd just discovered. Maybe it was not quite what we were looking for, but we honored the work and provided opportunities to emerging artists. We were offering a lot of what seemed almost forbidden pleasures in those times—jazz, experimental theater, political satire. Out of The New Ideas Program I eventually evolved the Brave New Workshop's guiding principles: "promiscuous hostility and positive neutrality."

With The New Ideas Program as the umbrella, there were soon three groups doing performances in my little theater, all working for no pay. The Ad Lib Ad Absurdum continued working with audience suggestions and improvisation in the mode of Word Jazz and Fliffus. It was my favorite.

The John Birch Society Players performed on Mondays

and leaned toward singing parodies and political songs with commentary in between. The third group was named The Brave New Workshop and performed written sketches. At the time, the newspaper people in town put on a yearly variety show called *The Gridiron Show*. When I sent out a call for scripts, several newspaper people showed up. That was how the first little group of writers and performers came in, including Irv Letofsky, Don Morrison, Dan Sullivan, and Gary (Garrison) Keillor. My old friend John Lewin—who would later join the Guthrie—also wrote sketches. John would put together a little revue production with his scripts, and then we would add improvisation. (I was calling it Instant Theater, and to qualify as Instant Theater, it needed to be connected to audience suggestions.)

It took all winter, but in June we had our opening night of "The Instant Theater Presents The New Ideas Program!" We started the show with the cannons of the *1812 Overture* and the sound of the espresso machine kicking out steam.

I knew from the circus that bill posting was the way to get attention for a show, so we slapped up a few hundred posters over one weekend. Dick Guindon used the red, white, and blue that became our signature colors after that. He painted a flag in the top corner and "SATIRE." "A BRAVE NEW WORKSHOP" was the headline. With posters all over town, we were no longer a secret. Overnight, people knew about the show. And they even bought tickets. The show was a hit, though still sloppy, and it was the beginning of using sketch scripts generated by that circle of writers.

This was a period in our history when improvisation

became a very small "i." When we split into our three little companies, the one that became most popular was not improvisational; it was scripted. But the feeling of the room and the style of production remained the same. I wanted "comedy theater for thinking people."

As the two other groups (Ad Lib Ad Absurdum and the John Birch Society Players) were absorbed into the Brave New Workshop, I decided to come up with a new show every month. This was the first time we had an "announced" schedule of shows, allowing an audience to plan. And the first time we had a format that so nicely jibed with my old newspaper routine from vaudeville. We could focus on one idea, satirize it, put up a bunch of sketches around it, and give the shows a revue structure of all-original material.

I remember almost constant recruitment, finding actors from the university and the drama program at Columbia Heights High School. Three of those kids became professional actors: Pat Proft, Mike McManus, and Tom Sherohman. Al Franken and Tom Davis also came into the Brave New Workshop through the recruitment of our summer youth programs.

I was mostly directing and producing. I enjoyed saying, "I now present . . ." like an Ed Sullivan of this little world. There was a range of tastes, but the scripts always had to have my approval before hitting the stage. By the time we moved to south Hennepin, the writers' list included about twenty-five people, and I was always busy selecting scripts that fit our mission.

With each move came an additional new audience, and

that tended to influence how we performed. Various pieces were artistically successful or got good reviews but didn't have sustainability for the audience. We wanted to be the loyal opposition to both political parties. Satirize everyone. Have no sacred cows, with no subjects off target. Our job was to mock and expose vice and folly.* Everything was fair game. And when an issue picked up momentum, we went with the momentum. I began to think of this approach to running a theater as "flying without a net."

---

* Some show titles were *The Vietnam Follies* (1966); *The Lyndon Frolics: Great Fables from the Great Society* (1967); *The Race Riot Review* (1967); *The Future Lies Just Ahead: The Watergate Story* (1972); *Bedtime for Reagonomics* (1983); *1984: Orswell That Ends Well* (1984); *What's So Funny about Being Female?* (1989/91); *Censorship of Fools; or, Jesse at the Helm* (1990); *The Recession Follies: BUSHwhacked* (1992); *Without a Clue: The Dumbing of America* (1994); *No Newt Is Good Newt: The Congressional Follies* (1995); *Campaign in the Neck: This Election Is Riggsed!* (1996); *Whose Lie Was It Anyway?* (1996); *Saving Clinton's Privates* (1998); and *Obama Mia* (2011).

★ 16 ★

THEATER WITHOUT A NET

"In this theater, we're not doing Shakespeare; we're not doing Chekhov. This is not meant to be great and lasting literature. What we're doing is found in this *performance only."*

Looking back, being able to walk onstage without rehearsal or a script, presenting material that is created at the very moment it is being performed—that was my goal. An actor's nightmare? No, my vision for Instant Theater.

Instant Theater was not instant. It took time to develop a way of working that actually worked. I kept looking for people willing to listen to just the possibility that this crazy Fliffus idea was not hatter-mad. I searched for actors and an audience who believed that there is joy and freedom in surprise, in knowing what the circus flyer knows—that a fall sharpens attention. No one wants gravity to win, but we are excited by the possibility. The flyer learns to succeed by rehearsing failure.

With Fliffus we learn to grow from our mistakes. We build on, add on, and improve the presentation. In the circus, we performed *with* a net. This was theater *without* a net.

For actors to trust each other and trust the process, we had to create an environment where they felt safe to improvise, to speak their ideas freely. Only then could Fliffus succeed.

We started generating scripts, and as soon as the actors merged into the writing process, the shows became more improvisational. Eventually, actors were expected to develop ideas, improvise in rehearsal, and write their own scripts. The Brave New Workshop went from being a "writer's theater" back to my original notion of an "actor/writer's theater" based on improvisation.

We had also developed a thinking audience, by ensuring that their ideas could be heard. It was all about trust and ideas, and doing things at the right time.

Every new show was ignited by some current event. In a way it was like the newspaper bit from my vaudeville act. In this case, I would provide a triggering word or concept. The actors would improvise around a big table in the basement, go home and write drafts, bring them back in, and we'd work it all again. They'd trade drafts with one another for rewriting until eventually I'd give the final OK on the production, which then continued to develop in rehearsal and performance as news changed. We were able to develop actors who could be fearless and able to think on their feet, and to fly "net free."

I was asking actors to make a jump from being "a moving chess piece" to barely controlled stage chaos.

And I was asking myself to try and control chaos. I was the title guy, the 3 × 5 index card guy, the triggering idea guy, and the director and producer. I developed what came to be called by others as the "Riggsian Rules." The number one rule: there is no rule. Unless it's this: "All ideas are welcome." To have good ideas, you had to have a lot of ideas—everyone's voice must be honored. Improvisation only works in a democracy. Our stated goal was to make everyone *else* look good. "We" not "me."

Ultimately, entertaining the audience was my primary goal. But alas, not all ideas work in a given production. Some ideas had to wait and grow before being performed. The idea was that all ideas are heard, but not all may make the cut. So there had to be someone to say: "We're not going to use your idea in this show." Once people believed that everyone's ideas would be considered—which in itself took some work—they then had to learn how to handle having their ideas denied, changed, delayed, or eliminated. Thankfully, they kept working.

And the theater thrived! Conditions at the time were ripe for us to shake things up. There was a somewhat repressive mood in Minneapolis when I first arrived; people were very proper and a little uptight. Anything after 10 p.m. was said to be sinful. All kinds of things were forbidden pleasures then. When we did our first shows, we practically had to explain what satire was. But in the circus I had learned that to be successful, I'd need to do something others were afraid to do.

Once we got into the 1960s, people were beginning to shake things up all over the country. And the Brave New Workshop happily began attracting a hip audience of people progressive enough to enjoy our shows. We found an audience willing to take a chance on a theater that was inventing itself. They came with an expectation of being entertained, but also offended. That is the balancing act: to enlighten *and* offend, but not so much that the audience won't come back. I used to say, "We want to make 'em laugh first, and then they fight about the issues on the way home."

Back when I first met Marylyn Rice, she asked me what I wanted to do with my life. I was pulled between pursuing a career in show business and a college education. Marylyn and I talked about a life in show business and the fact that there are defining limitations: (a) acts that are too expensive to mount, (b) acts no one wants to do because of the risk, and (c) acts you can only do if you have some immense special talent. I came from the tradition of "Let's do what everybody else is afraid to do." But what did this mean for me?

Grandmother Riggs had warned me about show-biz hyperbole: "Don't believe your own adjectives." I sometimes had the feeling that what we were doing could never be quite right, but it *was* right enough to continue. There were very few occasions when I'd look at the work and say, "I shouldn't be doing this." But then some guy walking by after the show would say quietly, "Mr. Riggs, you seem to have lost your way." And yes, the show didn't work that night. But he had been a fan for a long time, and so I'd think about it. Every time I thought I should shut the theater down, I realized I didn't want to throw away the audience that took years to develop or the actors who also took years to develop. Just when I considered quitting, some political outrage like Watergate or the frozen Congress would need to be addressed, I would see something in the news, and I'd think, "There's a show in that."

It's all a work in progress.

P. T. Barnum had long ago figured out a way of approaching the public that still has currency: The Greatest Show on Earth! The best slogan ever, even if it wasn't always the truth. So much about the circus depended on hyperbole and incredible grandiosity. With the Brave New Workshop, I wanted less hyperbole and as much truth as possible. That's what I saw in improvisation: truth comes from there, truth for that particular moment. While the old comedy traditions often denied truth, I wanted comedy to be funny because it *was* true.

In all our efforts to save the world from people who are always trying to save the world, there have been no sacred cows. Looking back at all the subjects and crises of the world that we satirized for laughs, I see that most remain today. The problems are still here. And we have more work to do.

I have always said, "In this theater, we're not doing Shakespeare; we're not doing Chekhov. This is not meant to be great and lasting literature." What we're doing is found in *this* performance only, *this* moment, *this* now. It should be funny, and it would have to be new, it would have to be brave. Brave and new!

But remember, nothing is sacred except the circus.

The height is not a problem. Even at this advanced age, my grip is still strong enough for solo work, though I do get a little winded going up the stairs. The aerial work I do now is not my personal best anymore, but it's well ahead of my personal worst. It's a secret (my secret), a necessary personal challenge—like my dad's habit of doing a handstand every morning.

My own private ritual—I try to keep it very cool. I look down from our tenth-floor balcony and see people on the sidewalk who are the right size to know that I'm above seventy feet—twice my flying-act elevation, half the altitude of my sway pole rigging. The steel rail is the same one-and-five-eighths-inch steel tubing I used for years, a very familiar size that feels good to my hands. Just think, I say to myself, I used to fly at this height.

My "civilian" friends never quite understand. High places make them nervous. A New York friend allowed me to see the view from his co-op on the fourteenth floor, and he said, "We don't use the balcony, I've lived here four years and have never been out there; I'm afraid I'd fall off . . . or jump."

A few years ago, I climbed the Sydney Harbor Bridge in

a self-guided tour of the solid steel girders 350 feet above the water. That gave a great lift to my spirits, the best I've felt in years. I'd do it every day if I lived in Australia and if getting there were not such a grind.

Why do I love to go high? I guess I just hunger for the top of things, not the competitive award-winning trophy top of things, but the sheer fun and ebullience of being up where most people fear to tread.

I try to not scare people by standing too close to the edge, and I try to avoid reminding them that there are some sensations that they will never ever feel. In these high-up quiet moments, I hear circus music in my mind's ear and feel the warm arousal of muscle memory just from pushing gently on the barrier. The exhilaration, the assurance, the feel of flying, comes back. I know that if I were offered a booking, I could still do the act.

ACKNOWLEDGMENTS

Why did I leave a successful life of show business glint and glamour to bring comedy improvisation (and espresso) to what was deemed "Flyover Land"?

"You should write a book." That was suggested often by hip friends, usually spoken in that moment right after I got caught reminiscing about all the wonderful events and life lessons learned during my early circus and show business life—Riggs family tradition, aerial energy, managed fear, joyful applause. Too often I was recounting the pride I felt in those wondrous years before I became a settled *towner.* And before the Brave New Workshop.

To Erik Anderson, my exceptional editor at the University of Minnesota Press, thank you for being someone who is really "with it."

Thanks to Rob Hubbard for writing the history of the Brave New Workshop *(Brave New Workshop: Promiscuous Hostility and Laughs in the Land of Loons)* and to Irv Letofsky (author of *Promiscuous Comedy).* Both freed me to write my own history as this memoir.

This book was years in the making. A very special thank you to Carol Mulligan, who was able to decipher my cursive, find the stories I had lost, and encouraged my use of correct spelling.

Thanks to my son, Paul Dudley Riggs, who with his mother, Ruth, were my early support in the development of the theater in Minneapolis.

Thanks also to Joshua Will, Carl Vigeland, David Tripp, Patricia Weaver Francisco, Stevie Ray, Dane Stauffer, Roxanne Sadovsky, Jim Lenfestey, and Paul Von Drasek.

I remain forever grateful to John Sweeney and Jenni Lilledahl for honoring the Brave New Workshop vision, and me, by creating thoughtful comedy and satire under my original banner of Positive Neutrality and Promiscuous Hostility. You and your company, led by artistic director Caleb McEwen, continue to make me proud.

Many thanks to Pauline Boss, my lovely wife, who has persistently encouraged me to publish my stories . . . since the early 1980s.

Dudley Riggs grew up in a distinguished show business family and has worked (since age five) as a vaudevillian, circus aerialist, clown, stage director, writer, and producer. A noted satirist of the daily news, Riggs is widely considered the father of improvisational theater. In the early 1950s, he created the Instant Theater Company in New York. In 1958, he founded the Brave New Workshop in Minneapolis—now the longest-running improvisational theater in the United States.

In 1987, Riggs received the Charlie Award from the National Association of Comedy Arts. In 2009, he received the Ivey Award for Lifetime Achievement for his significant contributions to the exceptional theater community in the Twin Cities. In addition, he received a Kudo Award from Twin Cities theater critics and the Urban Guerrilla Award. He lives in Minneapolis with his wife, Pauline Boss.

Al Franken began performing comedy in high school and was a featured performer at the Brave New Workshop before moving to New York to write for *Saturday Night Live* in 1975. He is the author of several books, and, in 2008, he was elected to the U.S. Senate, where he represents the state of Minnesota.